IF JESUS BUILT THE CHURCH

RETHINKING DISCIPLESHIP, THE POOR, & BIBLICAL SUCCESS

DERMOT COTTULI

Published by Cottuli Publishing Australia

ISBN: (Hardback) 978-1-7645376-3-6

ISBN (Paperback): 978-1-7645376-2-9

ISBN (eBook): 978-1-7645376-0-5

First edition

Scripture quotations are taken from the Holy Bible, New International Version (NIV), © 1973, 1978, 1984, 2011 by Biblica, Inc.™ Used by permission. All rights reserved worldwide.

Scripture quotations are also taken from the Holy Bible, New Living Translation® (NLT®), Copyright © 1996, 2004, 2015 by Tyndale House Foundation. Used by permission of Tyndale House Publishers, Inc., Carol Stream, Illinois 60188. All rights reserved

Unless otherwise noted, all Scripture quotations are the author's emphasis.

Cover design by Dermot Cottuli

Printed in Australia

This book is a work of non-fiction. All personal anecdotes are shared with permission or have been anonymised where necessary.

CONTENTS

CONTENTS

FOREWORD

Poverty and inequality are not decreasing realities in the Western world; they are intensifying.

Dermot Cottuli is a church pastor courageous enough to re-examine the KPIs of his church through the searching light of Scripture. As the book makes clear, this is not always a comfortable journey; it requires honesty, humility, and no small amount of bravery.

At Grace Church Clarence Plains, this re-evaluation led to the creation of a genuine "third place" for the community—something increasingly rare in our fragmented social landscape. This vision grew out of Dermot's deep theological conviction; something often described as God's "preferential option for the poor": the recognition that God's heart is especially attentive to those in need. Those of us born into relative comfort can miss this truth, insulated from the daily realities of vulnerability and scarcity.

Yet poverty and inequality are not decreasing realities in the Western world; they are intensifying. In

such a moment, churches cannot afford compla-
cency. If you want your church to be better equipped
to engage faithfully and courageously with the
growing inequality around us, this book will challenge and guide you.

We need a generation of leaders willing to wrestle
with the Scriptures, to sit with the uncomfortable
questions... and, like Dermot, who dare to measure
success by the standards of the Kingdom rather than
the metrics of the marketplace.

Dr Tanya Riches

*Director of Master of Transformational Development,
Eastern College Australia*

INTRODUCTION

We've been asking the wrong questions.

For nearly four decades, I've been involved in pastoral ministry, and for most of that time, I was focused on the usual metrics of success—attendance numbers, visitor retention, giving trends, and program participation. But ten years ago, after relocating our church to a social housing community in Southern Tasmania, we started to honestly grapple with this question:

"If our church were to close its doors tomorrow, would anyone in our community even notice?"

It's amazing what changes when you ask the right questions.

This book is the result of what we discovered when we stopped trying to build a successful church and started following Jesus into the places he actually went—to the poor, the marginalised, the forgotten, and the broken.

Some of what you'll read might make you feel uncomfortable. That's okay. We need our practice regularly challenged to see whether it aligns with the words of Jesus; otherwise, we run the risk of leading good people astray.

My hope is that this book will help you think more clearly about what it means to be the church and, in the process, see how the reality of God's love can change your local community for the better.

This book will have 3 possible outcomes for its readers.

1) It will reassure those who have felt that the current Sunday-centric focus of the church is lacking, and that the road that takes us to the poor, the oppressed, and the forgotten in our local communities is the one they'll find Jesus on.

2) It will provide a gentle course correction for those who have been lured onto a side road but still have a heartfelt love for Jesus and want His very best for their church.

3) It will act as a stop sign in the middle of the road for those pursuing a cultural Christianity that is quickly moving away from the teachings of Jesus and leading us toward a church that looks nothing like the example set by the poor, humble carpenter from Nazareth.

Who's the book for?

- Christians who sense there must be more to following Jesus than simply attending church.
- Pastors and leaders who feel uneasy measuring success by numbers alone.
- Churches longing to reflect Jesus more faithfully in their communities.
- Anyone willing to wrestle honestly with Scripture and uncomfortable questions.

You'll probably find this book raises more questions than it answers, but that's always been the pathway to our greatest seasons of growth—the pursuit of answers to questions which leave us stumped. At this moment in history, we need the courage to boldly ask questions that few in the Western church world are brave enough to ask, let alone answer. Which makes these the worst of times and the best of times to be serving Jesus.

"If your church closed its doors tomorrow... Would your neighbours grieve — or not even notice?"

Pastors, it's totally okay if you disagree with some of what's been written in this book, but if it helps you think more clearly about your practice, then it's a good thing. We're all pilgrims on a journey, which means there is always more to discover, and what one sees, another may not. Don't be afraid to ask questions, even if you feel you're disrespecting a sacred cow. We all see dimly as through a dark glass, but we have this confidence that the Holy Spirit will lead us into all truth. So, let's not stumble over the stones in the road but instead press on to take hold of all that Jesus has for us.

Introduction

CHAPTER 1

WAITING ON GOD – IT WILL CHANGE YOUR LIFE!

"Wait on your gift and always tell the truth."

— DC

I was two years into leading Grace, the church I'm currently pastoring, when I had a conversation with the Holy Spirit that changed my life in ways I wasn't expecting.

I was lying on our bed one evening listening to my wife talk about her experience at a recent conference and how the Holy Spirit had spoken to her, when a random thought popped into my head:

"If I want to grow our church, I really should ask the Holy Spirit how to do it."

I then proceeded to do just that, and immediately heard these words in my heart,

"Wait on your gift and always tell the truth."

Those words changed my life forever.

Neither of the two things I heard the Holy Spirit say that night fit within Church Growth 101 that I'd learned at Bible College back in the late 80s. It left me in a bit of a quandary as to what to do.

Not knowing what it meant to wait on my gift, I figured since the Holy Spirit was *the* Gift from God, I should probably try to spend concentrated time with Him on a weekly basis. To that end, I set an alarm on my Palm Treo (yes, I'm that old) to go off each Monday morning at 10 am with a note to go to the Botanical Gardens in our city and wait on the Holy Spirit.

That was my intention; however, reality was far different. Each week, Monday morning would roll around and at 10 am sharp, my alarm would buzz on my phone. I'd promptly turn it off and ignore it, as I always had way too much to do and felt I couldn't afford the time away from the office. This went on for nearly a year.

Every Monday morning my alarm would sound, and I'd turn it off and keep doing whatever work I was focused on at the time. However, like a grain of sand in a tight shoe, it gradually became increasingly aggravating until finally, one Monday morning, I hopped in my car and headed off to the Gardens for what would become my weekly routine for the next 6 years.

I found a garden seat off the beaten track, and every Monday morning at 10 am I'd make my way there and spend time learning what it meant to wait on God.

I figured if I was waiting on God, it wasn't an opportunity to tell Him about my previous or upcoming week, but rather a time to sit silently with Him, focusing my attention on Him. To do that, I would picture myself holding my heart silently in His presence. When I first started, I'd manage about ten seconds before my mind would wander, but over time, holding myself still in His presence became easier. It also became something I'd do at other times during the day, throughout the week. Whenever I had a moment of quiet, I found I could bring myself into His presence and sit with Him.

A few things I noticed.

Our church did grow during this time, even though there wasn't a direct correlation between my waiting on God and the things we did strategically at church. The only thing that may have been related was that early on in my journey of waiting, I felt a strong leading from the Holy Spirit to appoint Gus as my executive pastor. His friendship and unwavering support over the years has been a key factor in everything I've done as the senior pastor of Grace.

Secondly, it changed everything for me, both personally and ministry-wise, which, in the scheme of things, was far more important than my initial goal of church growth. My relationship with God became so much deeper. I learned that whenever I couldn't see a way forward, if I simply held the situation before God and waited on Him, He would always make a way.

So often in ministry, we don't know how to pray because we can't see everything clearly, but He can. Rather than telling God what I thought He should do, I found it far wiser to simply hold the person or situation before Him and, through my active waiting on Him, show that I trusted Him to lead me forward. It lowered the emotional heat of whatever situation I was facing and opened a door for God to move.

I found it easier to hear God's voice, and I felt far more secure trusting Him to come through in difficult situations. And slowly, oh so slowly, as I spent more and more time with Him, week after week, month after month, year after year, my experience of life and pastoral practice became increasingly aligned with His heart. That for me, has been one of the most precious outcomes of waiting on Him.

In the Tabernacle, when the fire on the altar burned, there was always a residue of ash left behind, which needed to be cleaned out regularly by the Levites. In ministry, there's always a residue of sin, pain, disappointment, and weariness that builds up over time and needs to be addressed, lest it get in the way of the work we're involved in.

A completely unexpected but very much appreciated byproduct of waiting on God was that as I spent time waiting on Him, my soul was gently cleansed, and it stopped the residue of life's disappointments from building up over time and causing issues.

I should point out that this process is ongoing; it never stops. The residue needs to be cleared out continually. Just as your car needs to be washed regularly to remove the dust it picks up from the roads it drives on, so too does your soul. If you make waiting on God a regular practice, you'll stay on top of any residue that builds up, and it won't become an issue for you later on down the track.

Having grown up in an era where I was taught that praying for at least an hour a day was the benchmark of true spirituality, I was shocked at the difference a few short minutes spent waiting on God could have on my inner world and outward ministry. In our pressurised lives, prayer can too often feel, more like a lobbing of requests over a wall, than a true meeting of hearts.

> *Brushing up against the divine and holding our hearts there in quietness and trust can't help but have a profound impact on our lives.*

He's waiting to be wanted...

Pastors, *when I first mapped out my book, I had this chapter right at the end because I wanted to get straight into it. I thought this chapter would be a nice way to smooth out some of the feathers I may have ruffled as we touched on a few sacred cows throughout the book. But then, as I reflected on my own journey, I realised this book would never have made it into your hands if I hadn't started the practice of waiting on God all those years ago. I hesitate to say this book is Spirit-inspired because I know myself and my own blind spots, but I pray He will use the words on these pages to renew your heart and give you courage to face the changes we all need to make to our practice, as we pursue His holy calling to shepherd His flock.*

     IF JESUS BUILT THE CHURCH

CHAPTER 2

THE EMPEROR HAS NO CLOTHES

Whilst it sounds nice to talk about revival, and it does seem to get people fired up, have you ever stopped to think that maybe we're just revving our cars in the garage without actually going anywhere?

— DC

OVER THE PAST 29 YEARS, I'VE BEEN ON A JOURNEY that began during my first stint as a senior pastor in Deeragun, an outer suburb of Townsville in North Queensland. In 1997, Debra and I headed north to take on the role as senior pastors of a 9-month-old church. Prior to Townsville, I'd spent 5 years in Tasmania helping to plant a church and then 4 years as an assistant pastor in Brisbane.

It was in Townsville where I first started to grapple with the question,

"What is it we're meant to be doing as pastors when we have the weighty responsibility of leading a church?"

I asked myself another question during our time in Deeragun and the answer to that question has since become a lifelong pursuit.

The question was,

"Where does Jesus want to be in our community?"

The answer I came up with at the time,

"He wants to be at the very heart of our community, not relegated to the fringes as he too often is."

Sounded great in my head, but how were we meant to take him there?

Obviously, if the church is his body, then it stood to reason our local church needed to be involved at a grassroots level in our community if our community were to have any hope of meeting Jesus through our service.

Which then led to another question,

"How would we know if we'd been successful in taking Jesus into our community?"

The only answer I could come up with was a new question,

"If our church were to close its doors tomorrow, would anyone even notice?"

I figured the answer to this question would show us if we'd been successful in reaching our community.

That last question has challenged my thinking and practice for nearly 3 decades now.

Over the last 10 years, it's morphed into:

"Would our community suffer if we were no longer around or would our absence make no difference whatsoever?"

We can talk about reaching the world, our nation, our state, or even our community till the cows come home, but if our community has no idea we're even around, all the praying in a back room won't change the relevance of Jesus to the average Australian.

Sure, God could send an angel to talk to people in their homes, but let's be honest, when has that ever happened in your experience? (*Be careful not to build your ministry expectation on the back of a testimony you watched on YouTube.*)

We can declare salvation over our neighbourhood and yell out *"Amen"* in our prayer meetings, but what difference does it make? Some say we're impacting the invisible realm, the realm of the supernatural, when we declare God's truth over nations. Now that may be the case, but then again, it may be making no difference whatsoever other than to drown out the quiet despair we keep hidden deep in our hearts when the reality of our experience doesn't measure up to our hyped-up expectation.

Am I saying I don't believe in prayer or prophecy? Absolutely not. But I'm more and more convinced that there's been a fair amount of prayer and prophecy over the years that has come more from well-intentioned wishful thinking than the leading of the Holy Spirit.

I love the movement I'm a part of, the Australian Christian Churches. I love the expression of Jesus' life and the prominence we've given to the work of the Holy Spirit in and through our local churches. But I'm starting to think we've stopped at the door and failed to enter into all that God wants for us — indeed, commands of us — in the great mission before us: reaching our communities with the love of Jesus. We speak a big game, but too often the substance is lacking.

If you attend a Pentecostal church, you've probably heard a message or two on revival, more so since COVID, I'm sure. Whilst it sounds nice to talk about revival, and it does seem to get people fired up, have you ever stopped to think that maybe we're just revving our cars in the garage without going anywhere?

The danger we face when talking about revival is that people will start to lose heart or, worse yet, their confidence in Jesus if what we're talking about on Sundays isn't happening in their day-to-day lives.

Hence, the challenging title of this chapter.

The anointing of the Holy Spirit wasn't given to believers so we could enjoy exciting meetings when we gather together for "church", but rather to enable us to go into situations within our community where *"angels fear to tread"* and young men *"stumble and fall."*

Jesus said he'd been anointed to take a message of hope to the poor. Peter said Jesus had been anointed by God and went around *"doing good and healing all those who were oppressed by the devil."* (Acts 10:37) It's what we're called to do. It's why the Holy Spirit anoints us.

Now I know Jesus taught about the Kingdom, but isn't it interesting that the first thing Peter remembered from his time with Jesus was that he went around *"doing good"*? And yet is this the message you hear from Pentecostal pulpits across Australia today?

Nowhere in scripture do we read that the anointing was solely for our own benefit. We don't find Paul or any of the other New Testament writers telling believers to pray for the revival of the church, and when they do pray for supernatural signs and wonders, it's in the context of being out in their communities doing what Jesus told them to do.

Ask yourself this question:

"When you pray for God to move, what exactly do you mean? What would it look like if He were to answer your prayer?"

William Booth, the founder of the Salvation Army, put it this way,

"I'm not waiting for a move of God; I am a move of God."

Maybe that's where our problem lies? We're not *moving* toward the poor, the vulnerable and the broken in our communities, the ones Jesus left the synagogue to reach.

How many poor or disadvantaged people do you know? Before you can preach, you have to reach; that's how we go *into* the world, but more on that later.

When you seek to help those worse off than yourself, you place yourself in the very position Jesus found himself in, and it's in this place where the true power of the Holy Spirit can be seen at work in people's lives.

Let's move out of our churches and into our communities and start doing them good. It's where Jesus is waiting for us.

CHAPTER 3

ANOINTED TO TAKE GOOD NEWS TO THE POOR

The anointing of the Holy Spirit was never meant to be an end in itself, but rather an empowering for mission, a mission which is seen in and through the good works we do in whatever community we find ourselves planted.

— DC

AFTER HIS BAPTISM, WHEN JESUS WAS LED INTO THE wilderness by the Spirit, Luke 4 says he was *full* of the Holy Spirit. When he came out of the wilderness after 40 days of fasting, we're told he came out in the *power* of the Spirit. It's at this stage in the narrative that our Pentecostal old-timers start getting excited.

Then Jesus heads back home and goes to his local synagogue on the sabbath. He's handed the scroll of Isaiah to read and starts reading from Isaiah 61—and the first words out of his mouth are, *"The Spirit of the Sovereign Lord is upon me, for the Lord has anointed me..."* (Luke 4:14). This is the bit we as Pentecostals love. But it doesn't stop there; Jesus then goes on to say *WHY* he's been anointed—*it's to bring good news to the poor.*

> *When he came to the village of Nazareth, his boyhood home, he went as usual to the synagogue on the Sabbath and stood up to read the Scriptures. The scroll of Isaiah the prophet was handed to him. He unrolled the scroll and found the place where this was written:*
>
> *'The Spirit of the Lord is upon me, **for he has anointed me to bring Good News to the poor**. He has sent me to proclaim that captives will be released, that the blind will see, that the oppressed will be set free, and that the time of the Lord's favour has come.'*
>
> *He rolled up the scroll, handed it back to the attendant, and sat down. All eyes in the synagogue looked at him intently. Then he began to speak to them. 'The Scripture you've just heard has been fulfilled this very day!'* (Luke 4:14-19)

Did you see that?

The very first group of people Jesus mentions are the poor, and he links his anointing by the Holy Spirit directly to his mission *to* the poor.

> *If the alleviation of poverty and injustice doesn't feature prominently in our churches' teaching*

*and practice, we risk being labelled hypocritical
in how we live out our stated beliefs in our
community. Similar to the accusations Jesus
levelled at the Pharisees of his day. If Jesus'
ministry was first and foremost to the poor, then
it's obvious the church is called to love the poor
first and foremost.*

If Jesus used Isaiah 61 as his missional mandate, how can we park ourselves at the anointing and not move on to the very reason the anointing is given: to reach the poor and the oppressed?

Could it be that the only true justification we have for the anointing of God's Spirit is when we're engaged in Jesus' mission to the poor?

> *Maybe it's not a lack of passion and desire for the
> gifts of the Spirit, but rather a lack of obedience to
> reach our communities through our good deeds,
> that's keeping us from seeing the miraculous,
> which was so evident in Jesus' ministry. That's
> something to think about...*

If the first port of call in Jesus' mission statement was the poor, why don't the poor receive top billing when Pastors gather to discuss ministry rather than strategies to grow our churches? Why don't Bible colleges make reaching the poor a priority in their training?

In all the time I've been a pastor, I've never attended a pastor's conference or engaged in ministry training where the poor were prioritised with the exception of Missions Conferences. What does that tell you? It's a glaring oversight, and one that the church needs to address, because *every* believer, not just the missionary, will be judged on how they treated the poor at the judgment seat of Christ. We can't just handball Isaiah 61 to our Missions department and feel we've done our job. Our responsibility to reach the poor needs to be front and centre in our church's mission statement.

The example of Jesus

Peter, when speaking to Cornelius' household after Jesus' ascension and the coming of the Holy Spirit on the fledgling church, said this about the Holy Spirit and the example Jesus set,

> *You know what has happened throughout the province of Judea, beginning in Galilee after the baptism that John preached—how God anointed Jesus of Nazareth with the Holy Spirit and power, and how he went around doing good and healing all who were under the power of the devil, because God was with him. (Acts 10:37-38)*

Directly after mentioning the anointing of the Holy Spirit that was on Jesus, Peter says Jesus went *"around doing good"*, and then he continues with *"and healing all those who were under the power of the devil."*

For Peter to bring up good works right out of the gate when talking to Cornelius shows us Jesus' reputation was built firstly on the good he did, *"You know..."* and *then* the supernatural power which was evidenced through the miracles following his ministry.

Some well-intentioned Pentecostals have at times skipped over the first part of Peter's statement and moved directly to the second part, overlooking something hidden in plain sight within the text.

When we lead with good works, people are more likely to open up to us and invite us into their world. It's at this point that they become much more receptive to our message of God's supernatural power to deliver them.

Later in John 13, when Jesus tells his disciples to love one another, he says that when they do, the world will know they are his disciples simply by the way they care for each other. Notice he didn't say, by their miracles or clever arguments, people would know, but rather by the way they treated those around them?

> *So now I am giving you a new commandment: Love each other. Just as I have loved you, you*

should love each other. Your love for one another will prove to the world that you are my disciples. (John 13:34-35)

That has to make you think...

Good works *and* the supernatural

Now, it's at this stage that some would say it's not either/or, good works or the supernatural, and I would absolutely agree. The supernatural manifestations we see through miracles and healings are proof that what we say about the Father and Jesus is true. Pentecostals have that right.

> *Then the disciples went out and preached everywhere, and the Lord worked with them and confirmed his word by the signs that accompanied it.* (Mark 16:20)

However, the supernatural was always meant to be a supporting pillar, not the focus, of our mission.

> *The mission of the church is to go to the poor, the marginalised, the downtrodden and those suffering injustice through no fault of their own, and through our good deeds and the good news of the gospel, point them toward Jesus' love for them.*

Some people have said that a gospel that leads with a focus on alleviating poverty and reversing societal injustice is a weak, woke version of the true gospel, and if we go down that path, we'll become irrelevant and miss our true call of making disciples of all nations. Yet Jesus says in Matthew 25:31-46, unless we feed the poor, give water to the thirsty, clothe the naked, open our homes to the homeless, care for the sick and visit those in prison, we won't gain entrance into heaven.

That can't be right, can it? If Jesus actually said this then why aren't we prioritising this message in our pulpits each Sunday? Well I'm glad you asked, because I don't know. Maybe you can answer that one for me?

Matthew 25 is a foretelling of a future event, not a parable. For church leaders, it's probably one of the most critical passages of Scripture in the New Testament to teach our people, because Jesus makes it very clear that all of us will be judged by the same criteria he uses to separate the sheep from the goats in verses 31-46, how well we loved people who couldn't repay us.

> *The Son of Man will come in all his glory. All the angels will come with him.*
>
> (This is a prophecy, not a parable)

Then he will sit in glory on his throne. All the nations will be gathered in front of him. He will separate the people into two groups. He will be like a shepherd who separates the sheep from the goats. He will put the sheep to his right and the goats to his left. Then the King will speak to those on his right. He will say, 'My Father has blessed you. Come and take what is yours. It is the kingdom prepared for you since the world was created.

I was hungry. And you gave me something to eat. I was thirsty. And you gave me something to drink. I was a stranger. And you invited me in. I needed clothes. And you gave them to me. I was sick. And you took care of me. I was in prison. And you came to visit me.

*Then the people who have **done what is right** will answer him.*

(Just stop here for a moment – Jesus has just told us what it is we should be doing with our lives)

'Lord,' they will ask, 'when did we see you hungry and feed you? When did we see you thirsty and give you something to drink? When did we see you as a stranger and invite you in? When did we see you needing clothes and give

them to you? When did we see you sick or in prison and go to visit you?'

*The King will reply, 'What I'm about to tell you is true. **Anything you did for one of the least important of these brothers and sisters of mine, you did for me.'***

(And then he talks to the goats)

"Then he will say to those on his left, 'You are cursed! Go away from me into the fire that burns forever. It has been prepared for the devil and his angels. I was hungry. But you gave me nothing to eat. I was thirsty. But you gave me nothing to drink. I was a stranger. But you did not invite me in. I needed clothes. But you did not give me any. I was sick and in prison. But you did not take care of me.'

They also will answer, 'Lord, when did we see you hungry or thirsty and not help you? When did we see you as a stranger or needing clothes or sick or in prison and not help you?'

He will reply, 'What I'm about to tell you is true. Anything you didn't do for one of the least important of these, you didn't do for me.'

*Then they will go away to be punished forever. **But those who have done what is right will receive eternal life.*** (Matthew 25:31-46)

If reading this prophecy from Jesus doesn't cause you to stop and think deeply about your own life and the things you consider of vital importance in your service to him, then I would question whether you're actually following him.

We need to seriously engage with these words of Jesus and allow them to shape the direction of our practice, or we run the risk of *"straining at gnats and swallowing camels"* and inadvertently leading our churches astray.

The Holy Spirit wasn't given to the church for the sole purpose of praying in tongues; the Holy Spirit was given to the church so we could go to the people Jesus went to, with a message of hope and a demonstration of God's love for them through our good deeds, both practical and supernatural.

What do you think is easier to do, praying in tongues or laying your life down for the least of these? By the way, laying your life down for another is the purest act of love you can demonstrate towards them.

If Jesus were looking at your life, which one would prove to him that you were listening to the Holy Spirit? Praying in tongues or loving the poor? Now I'm being a bit tough here, but it's for your own good. I want to challenge you to think more deeply about Jesus' priorities and how you can align your life as closely as possible with the things he's passionate about.

Be careful when you hear people say we're losing our Pentecostal distinctive when we don't focus on the gifts of the Spirit in a church service. As Paul said:

> *I thank God that I speak in tongues more than any of you. But in a church meeting, I would rather speak five understandable words to help others than ten thousand words in an unknown language. Dear brothers and sisters, don't be childish in your understanding of these things. Be innocent as babies when it comes to evil, but be mature in understanding matters of this kind.* (1 Corinthians 14:18-40)

This isn't just New Testament theology. You'll find similar teaching in the Old Testament—Isaiah Chapter 58 is a case in point.

God, through the Prophet Isaiah, was incredibly brutal in the response he gave to Israel's religious efforts, which they were taking great pride in at the time. All their praying, all their fasting, all their seeking of God when they gathered together was considered worthless because they weren't doing what God wanted them to do in alleviating poverty

and overturning the oppression that was all around
them.

> *Shout it aloud, do not hold back. Raise your
> voice like a trumpet. Declare to my people
> their rebellion and to the descendants of Jacob
> their sins. For day after day they seek me
> out; they seem eager to know my ways, as if
> they were a nation that does what is right
> and has not forsaken the commands of
> its God.*
>
> *They ask me for just decisions and seem eager for
> God to come near them.*
>
> *'Why have we fasted,' they say, 'and you have
> not seen it? Why have we humbled ourselves,
> and you have not noticed?'*
>
> *Yet on the day of your fasting, you do as you
> please and exploit all your workers. Your fasting
> ends in quarrelling and strife, and in striking
> each other with wicked fists. You cannot fast as
> you do today and expect your voice to be heard
> on high.*
>
> *Is this the kind of fast I have chosen, only a day
> for people to humble themselves? Is it only for
> bowing one's head like a reed and for lying in
> sackcloth and ashes? Is that what you call a fast,
> a day acceptable to the Lord?*

Is not this the kind of fasting I have chosen: to loose the chains of injustice and untie the cords of the yoke, to set the oppressed free and break every yoke? Is it not to share your food with the hungry and to provide the poor wanderer with shelter— when you see the naked, to clothe them, and not to turn away from your own flesh and blood?

Then your light will break forth like the dawn, and your healing will quickly appear; then your righteousness will go before you, and the glory of the Lord will be your rear guard.

Then you will call, and the Lord will answer; you will cry for help, and he will say: Here am I.

If you do away with the yoke of oppression, with the pointing finger and malicious talk, and if you spend yourselves on behalf of the hungry and satisfy the needs of the oppressed, then your light will rise in the darkness, and your night will become like the noonday.

The Lord will guide you always; he will satisfy your needs in a sun-scorched land and will strengthen your frame. You will be like a well-watered garden, like a spring whose waters never fail. Your people will rebuild the ancient ruins and will raise up the age-old foundations; you will be called Repairer of Broken Walls, Restorer of Streets with Dwellings. (Isaiah 58:1-12)

So very, very practical. You can't spiritualise any of this away...

Why did God get so angry with the Israelites? Maybe it was because their religious practices gave outsiders the impression they were close to God, but their day-to-day actions painted a picture of a God who was completely different to what He was really like.

> *When people outside of the church look at us, do they see us spending our treasure on ourselves or on the poor? Are we more interested in figuring out how to live our best life or laying our lives down for others so that they might live?*

When we compare this portion of Isaiah's prophecy with the prophecy of Jesus in Matthew 25, you can't help but realise they're related. The revelation of Isaiah and the prophecy of Jesus in Matthew go hand in hand.

Final Question

If being a disciple means following Jesus to those he's leading us to—the ones he prioritised in his earthly ministry—can you answer this question:

> *"Do you know who the poor and the oppressed are in your community?"*

If you can't answer this question, are you truly following him?

Or are you simply engaged in a religious practice that has no connection with the true ministry of our Servant King amongst the poor, the oppressed, the marginalised and the forgotten?

CHAPTER 4

WHY SHOULD THE CHURCH FOCUS ON THE POOR?

3.3 million people in Australia are living in poverty. Can you name one of them?

— DC

HAVE YOU EVER WONDERED WHY IT'S SO EASY TO identify the poor when overseas, but in our own country, it's so much harder? You're not alone. Our inability to read our own culture is one of the most challenging issues facing us as disciples of Jesus, because some of the values our culture holds run counter to the truth Jesus said would set us free. And if we're not aware of this, we can end up living so-called Christian lives that are lived in opposition to the truths Jesus taught.

In the West, two of our biggest cultural blind spots are individualism and materialism, and unfortunately, our churches aren't immune to their influence.

Individualism: we're taught from the cradle to the grave that our success in life is all about OUR personal accomplishments, fulfilling OUR dreams, finding OUR purpose, and living OUR best life. The main character in OUR story is ME.

Materialism: driven by insecurity and greed, it feeds back into our individualistic approach to life and our need for personal accomplishment. It's manifest in a constant pursuit of wealth to validate our sense of identity and secure our future.

> *Because of our cultural fixation on individualism and materialism, we very rarely consider the well-being of those around us as a prerequisite to our own flourishing.*

So, when Jesus comes along and says, *"sell your possessions and give to the poor"* (Luke 12:33-34) our individualism and materialism kick in, and we think, *"I need to protect what's mine. If I give away what I have, I will be less."*

Notice the focus is on what I have and how it impacts my identity. It's not just that *I'll **have** less*, but *I'll **be** less.*

The Western church then wraps it in pseudo-theology to justify holding onto our wealth and says things like, *"If I have nothing for myself, how can I be a blessing to others?"* Have you heard that one before or thought it yourself?

"I need to earn more so I can give more", can be a disguise for our individualism and materialism if we're not careful.

We take Scriptures like the one where God promises to bless the Israelites so they can be a blessing to the world (the Abrahamic covenant), and we use them to justify our pursuit of individual wealth, not realising we're feeding our cultural fixation with materialism and self.

And then along comes Jesus who says,

> *"Deny yourself, take up your cross daily and follow me. For the one who tries to save his life will lose it, but the one who loses his life for my sake will save it"* (Luke 9:23-24)

And we wonder why we struggle putting his words into practice.

> *We struggle to understand how to work this out in our lives because of the culture we live in, which has shaped how we feel and think about ourselves and the world around us.*

So how do we combat these cultural blind spots that we all struggle with? The Bible says quite clearly we do it by changing the way we think about ourselves and the things in life we pursue, whilst at the same time giving away our earthly treasure and laying our lives down for the benefit of others. Specifically, the poor, those suffering injustice, the outcast and the hurting. Those who are unable to pay us back.

If that doesn't cause you to wince, you're either really close to Jesus or you've hardened your heart to the voice of the Holy Spirit.

A young man who had accepted a traineeship working in our kitchen at the Grace Centre shared how thankful he was to Loaves and Fishes for giving him a job. When he applied for a job at the recently opened McDonald's takeaway in Glebe Hill, he said he was knocked back because he lived in Clarendon Vale, a social housing estate in Hobart.

Now, even though that may not have been the case, the message he internalised was that his identity and subsequent worth was lower than that of other young people from more affluent suburbs around our area. This belief about his identity, if left unaddressed, will limit his employment options and future life opportunities.

This is an example of the injustice perpetuated by the social system we live in here in the West, which determines worth and subsequent life opportunity, based on where a person lives, their family wealth and the privilege afforded them in society because of it; all of which this young man has no control over.

It takes away the power of choice for many of those living in social housing. They are often viewed as "troublemakers" and "slackers", unlike those from more affluent suburbs.

> *That view, when internalised, can have a detrimental impact on their sense of identity and their perceived place in society.* (Allen, K. A. 2019), (Kroger, J. 2017).

Left unaddressed, it narrows the range of opportunities available to them in life and locks them and future generations into a cycle of disadvantage and poverty, from which they feel powerless to break free.

Poverty goes to the heart of an individual's ability to make choices affecting their future well-being. It touches on all areas of life, including access to education, services, housing and medical assistance.

The World Bank estimates more than 700 million people are currently experiencing extreme poverty in the world today, which is an increase of 70 million people since the COVID pandemic in 2020.

Closer to home, Mission Australia estimates 3.3 million people in Australia are living in poverty.

- Two million "households" have experienced food insecurity in the last 12 months.
- One in six Australian children lives in poverty.
- Sole-parent families and renters over 65 years are the hardest hit by poverty.

When you look at those stats, I wonder if you can identify someone you know who would fit into one of those categories? Because, as we'll see later, these are the people Jesus came to reach, and if you don't personally know someone like that, then the chances of you reaching them are slim. Which then begs the question, are you truly following Jesus? *Ouch.*

> *When sitting around a dinner table with our friends, it's easy to wax eloquent about poverty and injustice as an abstract concept, but don't be fooled. There's always a real person on the other end of poverty and injustice. Neither can exist without victims.*

The Bible teaches us we were *ALL* created in the image of God (not just Christians and Jews), emphasising the dignity and "equal" value of every person

on the planet (Genesis 1:26, 27). If we truly understand the implications of this biblical truth—the
origin of everyone around us—it will profoundly
impact how we view and treat everyone in our
world. Regardless of whether they recognise it for
themselves, our understanding of this key truth will
shape how our churches interact with our communities and how we move through life and relate to
every person we meet.

**Just for a moment, I want you to think about
humanity from God's perspective.**

He created us all in his image. He considers us His
children. We all have equal value and worth in His
eyes. How do you think He feels when looking over
the earth and seeing the inequality and profound
injustice being perpetrated against so many of His
children by their brothers and sisters? His plan has
always been for us to be one, with everyone standing
shoulder to shoulder, not living in societies ruled by
hierarchical power structures where a minority hold
all the cards and the majority are left scrambling for
the scraps.

> *Poverty is not about numbers. It is about
> inequality, and specifically about inequality in
> power relationships. It is about a minority, less
> numerous, [who] performs all political func-
> tions, monopolises power and enjoys the advan-*

tages that power brings. (Jaykumar Christian, 1999)

So where did it all go so badly wrong?

To answer this question, we have to go right back to the beginning. Back to where it all started, the Garden of Eden. When Adam and Eve decided to place their own selfish desires on the throne of their heart, displacing their love for God with self-interest, the future of humanity was ensnared in a never-ending cycle of sin and death with no hope of escape until Jesus came. Through his death in our place, he provided for us the possibility of breaking the hold that sin had on all our lives.

In Genesis 3:17-19, we read that poverty, this struggle that so many are trapped in, was an outcome of the fall when sin entered the human race and impacted all of creation.

> *To Adam he said, 'Because you listened to your wife and ate fruit from the tree about which I commanded you, 'You must not eat from it,'*

> *'Cursed is the ground because of you; through painful toil you will eat food from it all the days of your life.*

> *It will produce thorns and thistles for you, and you will eat the plants of the field.*

By the sweat of your brow you will eat your food until you return to the ground, since from it you were taken; for dust you are and to dust you will return.' (Genesis 3:17-19)

It was never God's plan for humanity to live in poverty. His constant instruction to the Israelites, and later to the Church, around the alleviation of poverty, features prominently in all of God's redemptive efforts since the fall.

> *Poverty that results from injustice and exploitation is the most visible and striking sign of the sin of the world.* (Jaykumar Christian, 1999)

Throughout the Old Testament, God gave the Israelites strict instructions on how they should care for the poor, going so far as to say in Deuteronomy 15:4-5 there was no reason any Israelite should experience poverty, as His intention was to give them a land where there would be plenty for everyone.

> *However, **there need be no poor people among you**, for in the land the Lord your God is giving you to possess as your inheritance, he will richly bless you, if only you fully obey the Lord your God and are careful to follow all these commands I am giving you today.* (Deuteronomy 15:4-5)

Sounds amazing, doesn't it? But by the time Jesus turned up on the scene 1500 years later, poverty and injustice were commonplace in Israel.

> *The issue has never been the amount of resources available on the earth; the issue has always been centred around who has access to them and what they're doing with them.*

God was very explicit in his instructions to the Israelites regarding the way they were to treat those who were destitute with no one to defend them. He instructed His people to look after them and to take up their cause.

> *Learn to do right; seek justice. Defend the oppressed. Take up the cause of the fatherless; plead the case of the widow.* (Isaiah 1:17)

> *Speak up for those who cannot speak for themselves, for the rights of all who are destitute. Speak up and judge fairly; defend the rights of the poor and needy.* (Proverbs 31:8, 9)

The Israelites themselves experienced what it was like to be oppressed whilst living in a foreign nation because of their ethnicity, then subsequently being delivered out of the hand of their oppressors because of God's compassion toward them.

But the Egyptians mistreated us and made us suffer, subjecting us to harsh labour. Then we cried out to the Lord, the God of our ancestors, and the Lord heard our voice and saw our misery, toil and oppression. So the Lord brought us out of Egypt with a mighty hand and an outstretched arm, with great terror and with signs and wonders. He brought us to this place and gave us this land, a land flowing with milk and honey. (Deuteronomy 26:6-9)

Repeatedly throughout the Old Testament, we have references to God's heart toward the poor and those facing injustice.

He saves the needy from the sword in their mouth; he saves them from the clutches of the powerful. So the poor have hope, and injustice shuts its mouth. (Job 5:15-16)

When you reap the harvest of your land, do not reap to the very edges of your field or gather the gleanings of your harvest. Do not go over your vineyard a second time or pick up the grapes that have fallen. Leave them for the poor and the foreigner. I am the LORD your God. (Leviticus 19:9-10)

If anyone is poor among your fellow Israelites in any of the towns of the land the Lord your God is

*giving you, do not be hard-hearted or tightfisted
toward them.* (Deuteronomy 15:7)

*Whoever oppresses the poor shows contempt for
their Maker, but whoever is kind to the needy
honours God.* (Proverbs 14:31)

*Speak up for those who cannot speak for them-
selves, for the rights of all who are destitute.
Speak up and judge fairly; defend the rights of the
poor and needy.* (Proverbs 31:8-9)

*Woe to those who make unjust laws, to those who
issue oppressive decrees, to deprive the poor of
their rights and withhold justice from the
oppressed of my people, making widows their
prey and robbing the fatherless.* (Isaiah 10:1-2)

**God promises that those who look after the poor
will be blessed, demonstrating in a very tangible
way His concern for the poor and His intention
for his people to be involved with alleviating
poverty.**

*Give generously to the poor, not grudgingly, for
the Lord your God will bless you in everything
you do.* (Deuteronomy 15:10)

Now this next one is interesting because Jesus says in
Matthew 25 at the final judgement, *that when he was
hungry, we fed him,* when speaking of the poor.

*"Whoever is kind to the poor lends to the LORD,
and he will reward them for what they have
done." (Proverbs 19:17)*

**The poor won't repay you because they can't, but He
will....**

> *The generous will themselves be blessed, for they
> share their food with the poor. (Proverbs 22:9)*

> *And if you spend yourselves on behalf of the
> hungry and satisfy the needs of the oppressed,
> then your light will rise in the darkness, and your
> night will become like the noonday. (Isaiah
> 58:10)*

Disciples of Jesus are called to work towards a more
just and equitable society; it's part of being salt and
light wherever we find ourselves. This involves
addressing systemic issues that contribute to poverty,
such as corruption, unjust economic practices, and
discrimination.

The anointing of the Holy Spirit, which ushered in
the birth of the church, is directly linked to Jesus'
mission to the poor.

> *As we've already seen in our previous chapter,
> the first group of people Jesus mentioned in his
> missional mandate was the poor, and he links his*

anointing by the Holy Spirit directly to his mission to the poor. (Luke 4:14-19)

The Sermon on the Plain

Looking at his disciples, he said: 'Blessed are you who are poor, for yours is the kingdom of God. Blessed are you who hunger now, for you will be satisfied. Blessed are you who weep now, for you will laugh.' (Luke 6:20-21)

Do you realise Jesus wouldn't have said this unless there were poor people, hungry people, people in emotional distress, sitting in the crowd right there in front of him? And no, he wasn't talking about the poor in spirit; he was talking about those living in poverty, bound by systems they were powerless to escape from.

Far too many Christian leaders have used sloppy hermeneutics to justify their focus on their own economic demographic, saying that everyone is poor in spirit before Jesus. They then use this argument to excuse their failure to prioritise their responsibility to the poor. Jesus isn't interested in your demographic; he's only interested in the *"least of these"*.

In case you missed it in the previous chapter...

*If the alleviation of poverty and injustice doesn't
feature prominently in our churches' teaching
and practice, we risk being labelled hypocritical
in how we live out our stated beliefs in our
community. Similar to the accusations Jesus
levelled at the Pharisees of his day. If Jesus'
ministry was first and foremost to the poor, then
it's obvious the church is called to love the poor
first and foremost.*

But hey, knock yourself out and pick another target group that you're more comfortable with. Or better still, just say you're called to reach everyone equally. But make sure you're ready to explain to Jesus why you thought you knew better than him, *ouch*.

Jesus was very explicit in his teaching concerning his followers' responsibility to provide for the poor from their own means.

Disciples of Jesus are called to use their resources wisely and share with those in need. Our personal wealth is to be used for the benefit of others, particularly those living in poverty.

How would your church handle this next teaching of Jesus in Luke? It's way tougher than the usual version we use to teach stewardship in Matthew 6:19-21 because of how it starts.

This one's definitely an *"ouch"* for most of us.

Here's what I tell our church to do when they read something like this in their Bibles that they're not currently putting into practice. I tell them not to rush on to something more palatable but to sit with it and let the words of Jesus press up against their heart.

Over time, his word will change your heart if you give it the space it needs to soften your cultural bias and the fear that keeps you locked into self-preservation. This could take years; it has for me. I'm still not fully there, but I'm further down the road than I used to be. Be kind to yourself. The fact that life is a journey means you haven't arrived yet. Just make sure you're not actively avoiding the hard things Jesus said.

Luke, more than any of the other gospel writers, captured the heart of Jesus' teaching about the poor in a way you can't unsee once you've seen it.

*But when you give a banquet, invite the poor, the
crippled, the lame, the blind, and you will be
blessed. Although they cannot repay you, you
will be repaid at the resurrection of the righteous.*
(Luke 14:13-14)

The Bible speaks of the transformative power of the
Gospel. When we do things God's way, the consequences of sin are reversed, and we begin to walk in
the first fruits of God's future plan for our lives.

*Therefore, if anyone is in Christ, the new
creation has come: The old has gone, the new is
here!* (2 Corinthians 5:17)

**The sacred duty of the church is to see the poor set
free, transformed, and empowered through the
pursuit of equality and dignity for all, breaking
the cycle of poverty and enabling people to choose
their preferred future. A future where God's
priority for their lives is restored, and His Lordship is established.**

Revelation 21:4 says this about the future God has
planned for all who believe,

*He will wipe every tear from their eyes. There
will be no more death or mourning or crying or
pain, for the old order of things has passed away.*
(Revelation 21:4)

Poverty, along with every other outcome of sin, will be done away with when we're living fully within the Kingdom of God. In the meantime, we're to seek His Kingdom whilst here on earth, which manifests through a reversal of the impact of sin and poverty in whatever community our church finds itself in.

> *Poverty mars the identity of the poor and hurts the soul of all involved* (Jaykumar Christian, 1999).

CHAPTER 5

THE PASTOR'S RESPONSIBILITY TOWARD THEIR FLOCK

We all want to hear Jesus say, "Well done, good and faithful servant," when we stand before him. But what do we need to do here on earth so that he says those words when we finally see him face to face?

— DC

IF YOU'RE A PASTOR LIKE ME, I'M SURE YOU'RE extremely concerned about the words your people will hear when they finally stand before Jesus. What we want them to hear are the words, *"Well done, good and faithful servant."* (Matthew 25:23)

For Jesus to say those words, you need to know what it is he's looking for in the lives of his followers, then you need to teach, preach, equip and encourage your church to embody and practice the things Jesus is passionate about. If you do, and your people put into practice Jesus' commands, they will receive the warmest of welcomes into heaven in the future, and in the present, they will be transformed into his image, and your community will get to experience the love of Jesus in a profoundly personal way. *WIN WIN!*

What is Jesus looking for in the lives of his followers?

> *You are the salt of the earth. But what good is salt if it has lost its flavour? Can you make it salty again? It will be thrown out and trampled underfoot as worthless. "You are the light of the world —like a city on a hilltop that cannot be hidden. No one lights a lamp and then puts it under a basket. Instead, a lamp is placed on a stand, where it gives light to everyone in the house. **In the same way, let your good deeds shine out for all to see, so that everyone will praise your heavenly Father.** (Matthew 5:13-16)*

Our good deeds are salt and light!

Jesus is looking for good deeds that help the poor, the oppressed, the marginalised and the forgotten. Those good deeds will point people toward God.

I was at a pastor's retreat, sharing about the journey God had been leading us on as a church and the emphasis we were seeing in scripture to engage in good works for the poor, the oppressed, and the forgotten. One of the pastors who was there asked me how we could talk about good works without making our salvation dependent *on* them (a works-based gospel), because, as he pointed out, Paul said we were saved by faith, not by works, lest any man boast.

My reply to his question was, *"It's easy, we need to teach our people that their salvation is dependent on both, faith and good deeds."*

Now, before you cry *"Heretic"*, let me explain why I said that. I may not convince you that I'm right, but hopefully I'll help you to look at what you believe a bit more critically.

Paul *did* say in Ephesians 2 that we're saved by faith, not by works, and he was totally correct. Why? Because none of us is sinless and every one of us needs a sinless Jesus to pay the price of our sin so we can receive forgiveness. Salvation is a free gift that begins with the forgiveness of our sins. That's what Jesus dealt with on the cross through his death in place of us. We weren't able to do it for ourselves.

By trusting in him and in his sacrifice on our behalf, we receive forgiveness, and our sin no longer stands as a barrier between God and us. The door into God's presence is open, and we can walk boldly into his throne room as His adopted sons and daughters. None of us can die for our sins; Jesus had to do it for us, so in that regard, our salvation is totally free, a gift of grace.

If we were to die at the point of our profession of faith in Jesus, we would go straight to heaven, no problems whatsoever. The thief on the cross is a case in point. But if we remain on earth after our profession of faith, then *what we do and how we live our lives* becomes incredibly important to our future destination. This has nothing to do with the forgiveness of sin but everything to do with the Lordship of Jesus in our lives.

> *Your good deeds can't open the door of salvation; only Jesus can. But once it's open, it's your good deeds that will keep it from closing.*

The apostle Paul, who told us our salvation was a free gift from God, *also* wrote we can lose our salvation if we don't change our behaviour and persist in doing good, thereby proving through our actions that Jesus is truly our Lord.

> *But because of your stubbornness and your unrepentant heart, you are storing up wrath against yourself for the day of God's wrath, when his righteous judgment will be revealed. God 'will repay **each person** according to what they **have done.**' To those who **by persistence in doing good** seek glory, honour and immortality, **he will give eternal life.** But for those who are self-seeking and who reject the truth and follow*

evil, there will be wrath and anger. (Romans
2:5-8)

As we've already seen in Matthew 25, Jesus made it
clear that what we did for others was being recorded
and would be used to determine which side of the
line we'd find ourselves standing on when he
returns to judge our lives.

> *Then they will go away to be punished forever.*
> *But those who have **done what is right** will*
> *receive eternal life.* (Matthew 25:46)

Some people think that *"doing what is right"* is simply
believing in Jesus. The only way they can reach this
conclusion is by completely discounting what Jesus
had just been talking about in Matthew 25. Jesus was
very specific about the people we were to help, and
he made helping them the prerequisite for receiving
eternal life. His words, not mine.

This *"no responsibility"* gospel flies in the face of
Jesus' own teaching, in which he said, on multiple
occasions, that there are consequences for our
actions.

One such example, which should cause us all to sit
up and take note, was his teaching on forgiveness,
where he said, unless we forgive others, our Heav-
enly Father won't forgive us (Matthew 6:14). There's a

condition for you receiving "free" forgiveness: you're to offer forgiveness freely to others. To say you get a free pass to act in whatever way you like just because you believe in Jesus is a falsehood. But it wasn't just Jesus and Paul who said our good deeds were important.

James says our good deeds complete our faith, and without them, our faith is dead and useless.

> *What good is it, dear brothers and sisters, if you say you have faith but don't show it by your actions? Can that kind of faith save anyone? Suppose you see a brother or sister who has no food or clothing, and you say, 'Good-bye and have a good day; stay warm and eat well'—but then you don't give that person any food or cloth-ing. What good does that do?* **So you see, faith by itself isn't enough. Unless it produces good deeds, it is dead and useless.** *(James 2:14-17)*

> **You foolish person, do you want evidence that faith without deeds is useless?** *Was not our father Abraham considered righteous for what he did when he offered his son Isaac on the altar? You see that his faith and his actions were working together, and his faith was made complete by what he did. And the scripture was fulfilled that says, 'Abraham believed God, and it was credited to him as righteousness,' and he was*

 IF JESUS BUILT THE CHURCH

*called God's friend. **You see that a person is considered righteous by what they do and not by faith alone.** (James 2:20-24)*

It wasn't just Jesus, Paul and James who taught on this. The apostle John also drew the same connection between our faith and our deeds in his first letter.

*We know that we have come to know him **if we keep his commands.** Whoever says, 'I know him,' **but does not do what he commands** is a liar, and the truth is not in that person. But if **anyone obeys his word,** love for God is truly made complete in them. This is how we know we are in him: **Whoever claims to live in him must live as Jesus did.** (1 John 2:3-6)*

And then later in chapter 3 he says...

*This is how we know what love is: Jesus Christ laid down his life for us. And we ought to lay down our lives for our brothers and sisters. If anyone has material possessions and sees a brother or sister in need but has no pity on them, how can the love of God be in that person? **Dear children, let us not love with words or speech but with actions and in truth.** (1 John 3:16-18)*

As a pastor, you should constantly be teaching your church to do good and encourage them to love others better. If they put your teaching into practice, they'll hear Jesus say, "Well done, good and faithful servant." But if you neglect to teach them what Jesus requires of them, you'll be held accountable, as James is quick to point out in James 3:1.

Finally...

> *23 Let us hold tightly without wavering to the hope we affirm, for God can be trusted to keep his promise. **24 Let us think of ways to motivate one another to acts of love and good works.** 25 And let us not neglect our meeting together, as some people do, but encourage one another, especially now that the day of his return is drawing near.* (Hebrews 10:23-25)

Pastors, don't skip over verse 24 when teaching on these verses and go straight to verse 25. Verse 24 directly impacts a believer's eternity, whilst verse 25 is only helpful for the present.

CHAPTER 6

WHAT WE MEASURE WE START TO VALUE, AND WHAT WE VALUE DIRECTS OUR PRACTICE

When we stand before Jesus, he won't ask us for our tithe or our attendance records. But He WILL ask us if we've fed the hungry.

— DC

TOO OFTEN IN OUR CHURCHES, THE ONLY THINGS WE measure are bums on seats on Sunday, how much money was dropped in the offering, how many visitors we had over the weekend, how many volunteers we've engaged in each service and the number of small groups functioning throughout the week, along with the percentage of our people involved in them. Sound familiar?

Those measurements can then become the drivers of our practice—the why and the way we do church —and when that happens, we can find ourselves measuring our church's success against those key performance indicators (KPIs).

Can you see any issues that this driver of ministry development might cause within our churches?

When we use the "typical" church dashboard metrics as our measurements of success and then recruit our church members to meet those KPI's, we end up placing a burden on them that they were never meant to carry. Bringing people to church becomes the number one KPI that determines whether they're considered a *"good"* Christian, creating a class system that should never have gained any traction in Christian circles.

> *As long as pastors keep measuring their personal success by how large their church is, we will continue to produce stunted Christians who feel like failures.*

What should we be doing instead?

We should be discipling our church to obey the commands of Jesus, which isn't all that difficult when you think about it. There were only two, and the second proves the first according to John 14 and 15. We don't produce those disciples by preaching *our* job description to them, but by telling them what Jesus requires of them—the things he'll judge their lives by. And that always comes down to the good they do toward others, starting with the poor, as Matthew 25 so clearly tells us.

Fortunately (or unfortunately, depending on what you've given your life to), when we stand in front of Jesus, he won't be asking us for our tithe or our attendance records, or how many people we invited to church. He won't even be asking us how much time we spent in prayer each day or whether we memorised John 3:16. But He *WILL* ask us if we've fed the hungry, given water to the thirsty, clothed the naked, invited the stranger into our homes, cared for the sick and visited the prisoner.

I understand why pastors would measure bums on seats on a Sunday because they look out across their church each week and see every empty seat in their building. I understand why they might want to see those seats full rather than empty because it validates their ego and makes them feel good about their job and more confident when they hang out with other pastors (I'm being a bit mean here, but I promise if it helps you to change what it is you're measuring, it will be worth it).

The problem begins when we preach and teach in ways that pressure our people to fill our empty seats, and thereby cause them to measure their effectiveness and value as Jesus followers by the number of people they invite to our meetings.

Don't misunderstand me, I'm all for church growth. But even Jesus experienced ebbs and flows in the number of people who followed his ministry. It didn't affect him because he knew his mission, and his mission was far more important than the fickleness of the crowds following him.

Jesus has so much more he wants to do through our people in their world during the week, but if we limit them by teaching a stunted version of church-centric service, we hamstring the greatest asset he has.

Their place of ministry is in their homes, schools, and workplaces—the places they find themselves in naturally throughout their week.

Our church services were never meant to be the main game; the main game is played from Monday to Saturday wherever we find ourselves living during the week. Our church services are the change sheds our teams retire to for a breather between sessions of play.

Which brings us back to a very important question...

"What is it you're measuring in your church?"

Answer that question, and you'll reveal your personal KPIs. You'll open a window into why you're doing what you're doing and what the driver behind your practice is. It's only when we face up to what's driving us that we have any hope of changing our motive, direction and ultimately our destination.

CHAPTER 7

IS IT BETTER TO REACH BEFORE YOU PREACH?

"Go into all the world..." How do you do that? Not by praying. Not by preaching. You do it by reaching.

— DC

SOME PEOPLE HAVE SAID COMMUNITY ENGAGEMENT IS my thing, but that's not actually true. My thing has always been Jesus and His church.

Specifically, knowing what Jesus wants us to do as pastors and church leaders, and how his priorities should shape our practice.

However, given what I just said, community engagement probably is my thing because it's the first part of the Great Commission. *"Go into all the world ...."* (Mark 16:15)

How do you go into all the world?

You don't do it by praying, and you don't do it by preaching. They're the bookends to the *"go"* part. You do it by reaching the community you've been planted in and letting them experience something they've never experienced before—the love of Jesus expressed through your good works.

Before you preach, you have to reach, but how do you reach?

You reach by doing what Jesus did: serving others, specifically the poor, the marginalised, the broken and the outcast.

In 2016, our church moved into Rokeby, Clarence Plains, a social housing estate on the eastern shore of the Derwent River in Hobart. We bought an old, rundown pub, and right from the beginning, we decided we wouldn't start any programs or advertise our church in our community. Instead, we'd find out what our community was already doing and offer to help them do what they thought was important. (That's how service became our entry point into Clarence Plains.)

We decided not to hold church services on our property but instead offer it as our gift to our local community. We wanted them to be able to test drive the love of Jesus without any strings attached. To make that happen, we had to hire a local school hall for Sunday services. We felt it was worth the cost, as no one could then accuse us of using our building as a bait-and-switch tactic. And yes, that's a criticism that gets levelled at churches by our communities more than it should.

This is what we discovered—when you truly try to serve your community with no strings attached, doors will open for you without you having to knock. And because you're there with your community when those doors open, all sorts of opportunities present themselves. When you genuinely love your community through your presence and service, your community will open its heart to you. It's human nature. When we know people genuinely care for us, we let down our barriers.

We've faced zero resistance from our community in all the time we've been in Rokeby because we were willing to set aside our own agenda and come alongside the people who live there to help them achieve their goals.

If you try to preach before you've reached, you'll come up against a brick wall eight times out of ten, and it won't be the devil. It's the way people work. Nobody likes being told what to do by people who are different to them. Ever had your door knocked on by a Jehovah's Witness? If so, you'll know what I'm talking about.

So, armed with an attitude of serving our community's agenda rather than running programs ourselves, we had a discussion with Loaves and Fishes in 2018, offering them space at our old pub for a southern production kitchen. They already had a kitchen provided for them by Housing Tasmania up north of the state, and they needed one down south.

Loaves and Fishes had taken over Second Bite in Tasmania a few years earlier and realised many of the people they were providing fresh food for didn't know how to cook meals with the food products they were receiving. So they decided they would take the food and cook ready-to-eat meals that were nutritious and healthy, then distribute the meals through their network, which spanned nearly 300 community groups right across Tasmania. They were soon churning out thousands of meals a week.

The interesting thing about their model is they give the meals to community groups, who then distribute the meals to those in need. Loaves and Fishes aren't even seen at a distribution level; it's the community group that gets the kudos.

A Kingdom principle, if ever there was one.

> *Be careful not to practice your righteousness in front of others to be seen by them. If you do, you will have no reward from your Father in heaven.*
>
> *So when you give to the needy, do not announce it with trumpets, as the hypocrites do in the synagogues and on the streets, to be honoured by others. Truly I tell you, they have received their reward in full. But when you give to the*

needy, do not let your left hand know what your right hand is doing, so that your giving may be in secret. Then your Father, who sees what is done in secret, will reward you.
(Matthew 6:1-4)

Well, back to our old pub and more than half a million dollars later (that's a miraculous story of provision in itself) and a lot of hard work, on the 14th of February 2023, Loaves and Fishes started cooking meals for Tasmanians doing it tough out of their brand-new southern production kitchen based at the Grace Centre in Rokeby. 2500 cooked meals are prepared and delivered from their southern kitchen each week, and 4 young people from our local high school are doing traineeships in food preparation and handling.

> *If you're not worried about seeing your name up in lights, serving others is a no-brainer; everybody benefits, especially your community and your church's reputation.*

You've probably realised this type of approach takes time. You have to winter and summer with your community over multiple years to prove to them you're genuine, but there's something wonderful happening in the background during that time. As your relationship strengthens, their resistance to

Jesus diminishes because they've been able to road test his love for them through your authentic service.

The journey never ends, which is why service can't just be a tool you use. It has to be embedded in the very nature of your church just as it was in the character of Jesus. Then, regardless of what return you receive for your service, you'll keep living it out.

I'd like to finish this chapter with one last thought that may, for some of you, be a little challenging, but I think most readers of this book will understand what I'm trying to say; it's pure Bible, after all.

This is where I've landed after nearly 4 decades of church ministry. This is what Andrew Hillier (the CEO of Loaves and Fishes) and I talk about all the time. I'm sure it will resonate with every senior pastor reading this and also those with a heart for his church.

The world isn't looking for a successful, powerful, all-conquering church. The world is looking for a church that looks like Jesus, our servant King.

- A church that will love them authentically through their presence with them and their service to them.
- A church that will prove to them they're worth dying for.

- A church that's willing to sacrifice its treasure for the hungry, the homeless, those in prison, and those society shuns. Not just simply using it for the building of places of worship for itself, but also in reaching out and caring for those that everyone else forgets.
- A church that's willing to lay down its own agenda and follow Jesus wherever he leads them. *(If you're following Jesus, you will find yourself amongst the poor, the hungry, the broken, the refugee, the forgotten and the overlooked. And if you don't, are you even following Jesus?)*

This is the love that overcomes the world. This is the love that leaves them undone.

- This is the love that our Saviour demonstrated when He left heaven and lived amongst the poor, the outcast, the powerless and the weak.
- This is the love that saw Him lay down his life for every single person on the planet, not just the Jews.
- This is the love He's offering us and asking us to share with the communities we're planted in.

- This is the love that opens wide the door to our salvation.

CHAPTER 8

MY DILEMMA WITH DISCIPLESHIP

"Go and make disciples of all nations." Is this the responsibility of every single believer, or just those who have been gifted to do so?

— DC

Then the eleven disciples went to Galilee, to the mountain where Jesus had told them to go. When they saw him, they worshiped him; but some doubted. Then Jesus came to them and said, "All authority in heaven and on earth has been given to me. Therefore go and make disciples of all nations, baptising them in the name of the Father and of the Son and of the Holy Spirit, and teaching them to obey everything I have commanded you. And surely I am with you always, to the very end of the age. (Mathew 28:16- 20)

IF YOU'VE GROWN UP IN AN EVANGELICAL OR Pentecostal church, you've most likely heard that the greatest responsibility of any believer is to *"Go and make disciples!"* Southern Baptist Pastor Rick Warren coined the famous phrase, *"A great commitment to the great commission and the great commandment grows a great church."* I've heard people say from pulpits we're all meant to be *"Disciples who make disciples."* It's a nice catchy slogan, but is it true?

The making of disciples in many churches has been pushed as the penultimate act of Christian service. I understand why people would think that, after all, it was the last command Jesus gave to 11 of his disciples before ascending to heaven. But increasingly I'm starting to believe we've missed something important, and our churches have suffered because of it.

> *It's very difficult to read our Bibles without being influenced by our cultural and denominational biases. There are so many things we take as self-evident because that's what we were brought up believing. Changing the way we think about them can be incredibly challenging. This injunction to go and make disciples is a case in point.*

Now, there's no argument that making disciples of all nations is the mission of the church as a whole, but the question we need to tackle is whether it's the responsibility of every single believer or only those who have been gifted to do so.

Why is it important to address this question?

It's important because our answer to this question directly influences what we teach in our churches. In particular, how we expect a believer to behave. If we teach that the church expects every believer to make disciples, we then have to prove that everyone can. This chapter questions whether that's possible.

Let's start with Jesus' command to go and make disciples of all nations.

The question we need to answer is:

"Who was he talking to when he gave this command?"

We know there were hundreds of committed believers at this stage, many of whom had seen Jesus resurrected. Paul mentions that Jesus appeared to 500 brothers and sisters at the same time, after his resurrection. And yet there were only 11 disciples with Jesus when he gave the command to go and make disciples of all nations. Now that doesn't mean they weren't then meant to pass it on to others, but have you ever wondered why, when you read through the Epistles, Paul, Peter, James and John don't highlight the making of disciples by all believers?

> *If making disciples is the primary duty of every believer, then surely it would be scattered*

What we repeatedly find in the Epistles are instructions to believers on how to act toward others in love, along with a constant injunction to stop sinning and live righteously. If making disciples were the number one priority for every believer, wouldn't it get the same amount of airtime as doing good works?

Could it be we've taken a missional command given to some and made it an institutional command to all?

Is it possible that there are people within the body who are gifted to teach and therefore have a responsibility to do just that, teach believers what it is to be a disciple of Jesus?

According to Jesus, teaching is an integral part of making a disciple "...*teach them to obey everything I have commanded you...*" And yet, in his letter to the Jewish diaspora, James discourages believers from becoming teachers: *"Not many of you should become teachers, my fellow believers, because you know that we who teach will be judged more strictly."* (James 3:1)

If the making of disciples is the duty of all Christians, then James is clearly out of step with Jesus' command.

Now, whilst most people can sing, we wouldn't tell everyone they have to audition for The Voice (we've all seen those embarrassing auditions on TV). Neither would we expect everyone in our church to be able to stand before a group of strangers and teach on the difference between the Old and New Covenants simply because they can talk. I know how to run, but there's no expectation that I'd be as fast as Usain Bolt over 100m.

But what if we lived in a society where everyone was expected to sing and speak in public on a stage, regardless of their ability, gifts, or personality? That would be totally unfair, wouldn't it? We'd think it was ridiculous and cruel, and we'd call it out. For something to be expected of everyone means everyone can do it.

Paul picks up on this topic in his discourse about the body when he talks about the different gifts we each have in 1 Corinthians 12 and Romans 12. He says we all have different gifts and we shouldn't think everyone will be the same.

Paul has no expectation that everyone will have the same gift and, correspondingly, the same responsibility within the body. It's why we don't teach that everyone has to do the work of an apostle, a prophet, an evangelist, a teacher or a pastor.

Now we can all sing, talk, and run; we can all share our faith, encourage others to do good, and read our Bibles with our friends, but to expect we can do the same things that Paul did, according to the gift that was on his life, would be foolish unless we had the same gift on ours.

What we can all do is share the hope we have when we're asked. Peter tells us to be ready to do just that when a question is asked of us about the hope that we have.

> *But in your hearts revere Christ as Lord. Always be prepared to give an answer to everyone who asks you to give the reason for the hope that you have. But do this with gentleness and respect.* (1 Peter 3:15)

But this is quite different from what the 11 apostles did after receiving Jesus' command to go into all the world and make disciples.

Contrary to what some teach, we're not *all* called to be an evangelist. In fact, I would suggest one of the reasons the church is seen in an unfavourable light at times is because we have people trying to do things they aren't gifted to do.

But what about Timothy? Didn't Paul tell him to *"do the work of an evangelist?"* I'm glad you asked. Let's look at what Paul told Timothy.

But you, keep your head in all situations, endure hardship, do the work of an evangelist, discharge all the duties of your ministry. (2 Timothy 4:5)

It's commonly believed Timothy had an ascension gift ministry, one of the 5 ministry gifts Paul mentions in Ephesians 4 for the equipping of the church for works of service. Paul is telling Timothy to discharge all the duties of his ministry. What ministry? The ministry of an evangelist.

Just for a moment, let's change the recipient of Paul's instruction and imagine Paul is writing to Peter, instead of Timothy. If he had said, *"Peter, keep your head in all situations, endure hardship, do the work of an apostle, discharge all the duties of your ministry."* What duties would you assume Paul was referring to? The duties of an apostle obviously. The Ephesians 4 ministries are given to individuals and are not expected of everyone.

> *Now ask yourself: what does the Bible say we will ALL be accountable for when Jesus judges our lives? Then teach that as the responsibility of all.*

Go back and read Matthew 25:31-46 if you've forgotten. Jesus is crystal clear—we'll *ALL* be judged on whether we fed the hungry, gave water to the thirsty, welcomed the stranger, clothed the naked, cared for the sick and visited prisoners.

Not once does he mention any of the things we equate with being a *"good disciple"* in your typical Western church. Instead, Jesus very clearly states we will *ALL* be judged on how we treated the poor, the homeless, the sick and those in prison. We are *ALL* called to love them in action and not just in thought.

> *There IS something we're ALL called to do. We're all called to love those who can't repay us. Who are those people? The hungry, the thirsty, the naked, the homeless, the sick and those in prison.*

I want you to imagine what it would be like if everyone in our churches believed that doing good was the number one responsibility of every believer, and it was the main thing Jesus would be judging the fruitfulness of their lives against. What type of impact do you think the church would be having in our communities if that were the case? How prepared would the soil be for the gospel when those who are gifted to speak and make disciples start to teach?

Pastors, don't fall into the trap of preaching your job description to your congregation. There are those in our churches who are responsible for making disci-ples, and you're most likely one of them. They've been called and gifted to do it, but not everyone is in the same boat. It doesn't mean people can't encourage their friends to obey Jesus's commands; we all should. But our callings and gifts are unique, and we're only responsible for what we've received.

(And I haven't even started to discuss the other elephant in the room, how so often in the evangelical church world we confuse conversion with discipleship. The Holy Spirit is the author and instigator of every conversion. Our responsibility is to then see the converted become disciples, people who obey the commands of Jesus.)

> *Let's teach what the Bible actually says, and let's emphasise the things our people are dying to know, lest they die not knowing.*

Well done on getting to the end of this chapter; it could be considered mildly or radically controversial depending on what you've been taught in your church. That's okay. If it helps you to think more rigorously about your current practice, that's a good thing; no one ever starts off seeing the entire picture. It's a bit like putting a jigsaw puzzle together without the picture on the box to help you. You start off focusing on certain aspects of the puzzle that make sense to you. It could be a bridge or a tree or just the straight outside edges, but over time, as you fill in more of the puzzle, you start to realise the things you focused on

originally may not have been the central point of the puzzle in the first place. It doesn't mean the things you initially focused on were wrong. It just means there's more to the picture than you can currently see. Over time, as you continue walking with Jesus, what is truly important will become far more obvious than what you first saw when starting your journey.

CHAPTER 9

IT'S FAR SIMPLER THAN YOU THINK

A disciple is someone who has been baptised and obeys the commands of Jesus. That's it.

— DC

Therefore, go and make disciples of all nations, baptising them in the name of the Father and of the Son and of the Holy Spirit, and teaching them to obey everything I have commanded you. And surely I am with you always, to the very end of the age. (Matthew 28:19, 20)

IT'S PRETTY OBVIOUS FROM THE ABOVE THAT THE church's mission is to make disciples in all the nations of the earth. But there seems to be a lot of confusion in the church world today about what a disciple is. It's become a bit of a trending topic in recent years, which I find a bit confusing, to be honest. After all, Jesus' teaching on discipleship was simple, straight to the point and easy to remember. And yet his simple teaching had the power to shape and grow us for the rest of our lives if we put it into practice.

What was Jesus' definition of a disciple?

A disciple is someone who's been baptised and obeys his commands.

That's fairly straightforward, isn't it?

Which leads us to the next question we should ask:

"What are the commands of Jesus?"

Not the bylaws of your church, your denomination or your church leadership team, but the commands Jesus gave to his disciples.

Jesus made it easy for us when he summed up all the commandments of God in just two, which he said are of equal importance.

> *Teacher, which is the most important commandment in the law of Moses?"*
>
> *Jesus replied, 'You must love the Lord your God with all your heart, all your soul, and all your mind.' This is the first and greatest commandment. A second is equally important: 'Love your neighbour as yourself.' The entire law and all the demands of the prophets are based on these two commandments. (Matthew 22:36-40 NLT)*

Jesus then expands on this in John 13:34, where he says we're to *love one another as he has loved us.*

He then ties the first and second commandments together when he says in John 14:15, 21 and 23 that **"..if we love him, we will obey his command",** which he then clearly spells out toward the end of this particular conversation with his disciples in John 15:12:

> *My command is this: Love each other as I have loved you.* (John 15:12)

Which brings us to this startling conclusion:

Jesus measures our love for him by how well we love others.

Have you ever seen that before?

It's here we see the genius of Jesus on display. It's easy to say you love God, but it's only when you lay your own life down to love others that it's proven genuine—according to Jesus.

What did Jesus do for us here?

He outlined the pathway to personal transformation.

Discipleship is meant to develop the nature and character of Jesus in your life. Due to your sin nature, that process hurts. Why? Because you have to deny yourself to love others, and in doing so, you start to understand what it means to take up your cross daily as you follow him.

Jesus said if we really love him, we'll do it. And when we do it over and over again, we are transformed into his image.

The number one goal of any type of discipleship is that we end up looking like the master we follow.

Which is why Jesus said in John 13, *"If you love each other the same way I have loved you, you will look like me, and people will know that you are my disciples." (My paraphrase)*

It's profoundly simple and simply profound!

> *So, to be really concise, a disciple is someone who obeys Jesus' commands.*

If you want to make a disciple of Jesus, your primary goal is to help them grow in obeying Jesus' command to love others as Jesus has loved them, full stop.

You can't call yourself a disciple of Jesus if you aren't obeying his commands?

What's the difference between this method of making disciples and the way we've been taught in our churches?

For starters, I didn't say we need to get them to read their Bibles and pray each day. I didn't mention church attendance, tithing, or volunteering in a church ministry, which are common components of a typical discipleship program.

Why is that?

Because Jesus isn't coming back to judge any of those things. He's only going to judge their lives against how well they loved the poor, the homeless, the sick and the imprisoned. So it's imperative that we start with his commands and *then* move on to the things that will benefit them personally.

When we get this pattern back to front, we end up creating all sorts of issues for new believers and their relationship with God, their understanding of themselves, and what they then give their lives to.

Unfortunately, we get it back to front far too often. To the extent that in most churches today we measure a person's spirituality by how much they pray and how much of the Bible they know. Which flies in the face of what Jesus and the New Testament writers actually taught—that a disciple is someone who obeys Jesus' command to love others as he has loved them.

The Apostle John couldn't spell it out any clearer for us when he wrote these words in his first letter...

And we can be sure that we know him if we obey his commandments. If someone claims, "I know God," but doesn't obey God's commandments, that person is a liar and is not living in the truth. But those who obey God's word truly show how completely they love him. That is how we know we are living in him. Those who say they live in God should live their lives as Jesus did. (1 John 2:3-6)

Spiritual people obey Jesus' commands.

Go and Google what people think a godly person looks like, and you'll find most of the results will describe a person who prays, reads their Bible, attends church services, and tithes. You'll be hard-pressed to find a godly person described as someone who obeys the commands of Jesus. And yet that's the only thing Jesus is concerned about when he looks at our lives: how well we love the people in our world who can't repay us.

As soon as possible, we need to start teaching new believers that Jesus is primarily concerned with how they treat the people in their world and encourage them to start doing good to all the people around them, enemies included.

Jesus didn't say wait till you know more before you start loving others. He didn't say wait until you're emotionally healed before you start loving others.

He didn't even say wait till you know how much you're loved by God before you start loving others, and he most definitely didn't say you need to feel good about yourself first, before you start loving others.

Why?

Because Jesus, being the wisest teacher who's ever walked the earth, knew that when we obey his command to love others, *we* begin to transform on the inside. The self is dethroned, and we begin the process of healing our own soul. The very act of loving others brings about a change in our own inner world. Is it any wonder Jesus never said, *"Go and find someone to love you and you'll be healed."* Instead, he said, *"If you love me, obey my command. And this is my command, love each other as I have already loved you."*

The truth is, any Christian I've ever known who has actively made loving others their primary goal in life ends up practising all the other Christian disciplines anyway. They have to, because when we're sacrificially laying our lives down for others, we'll find ourselves on our knees constantly, reading our Bibles as often as possible and hanging out regularly with other Christians because we soon realise, we need all the help we can get to love others the way Jesus is calling us to love.

Maybe that's why Jesus won't be judging us on how well we incorporate spiritual disciplines into our lives, because *WE* benefit from them. It's only when we consistently love those who can't repay us that all of heaven sits up and takes notice. Why? Because the self has been de-throned and Jesus' commands are directing our lives. That's when you know you're dealing with a genuine disciple.

> *So Christ himself gave the apostles, the prophets, the evangelists, the pastors and teachers, to equip his people for works of service.* (Ephesians 4:11-12)

Our job as Pastors is to equip believers for works of service. Service is simply love in action. Therefore, our job is to teach our people how to love others better, over and over again.

We do our churches a huge disservice when we make their service primarily about serving on a team at our weekly Sunday meetings. Serving on a team on Sunday is like doing chores at home. Someone has to do them, but seriously, if you think they're going to change the world, you really need to get out more.

The love that changes the world is the love that reaches down to care for the poor, the oppressed, the marginalised and the forgotten, day in and day out.

So, by all means, teach your church how to pray, why
they should read their Bibles regularly, the benefits
of church attendance and regular giving, but don't
think for a minute that someone who does those
things consistently is a disciple of Jesus. They may or
may not be. A true disciple of Jesus is someone who
obeys Jesus' command to love others, over and over
again.

The typical church things I mentioned above benefit
the believer, but obeying Jesus' command to love
others costs the believer, sometimes with no visible
return at all.

You can imagine which one is the easiest to get
people to do—the one with the personal benefit
attached. But if you dare take the narrow road, the
road less travelled and teach your church to obey the
commands of Jesus first and foremost, you will have
fulfilled his call to make disciples and helped your
people to live the life Jesus died for them to have.

Pastors, *that got quite serious near the end, didn't it? Just to be clear, I'm not saying people shouldn't know what's in their Bibles. I'm saying people should know what's in their Bibles, but I don't think we do. Otherwise, we'd know what's most important to Jesus. And knowing what's most important to Jesus would then dictate what we teach from our pulpits and directly influence what our churches look like to our communities.*

CHAPTER 10

WHO WOULD
JESUS SIT WITH?

"Why does your teacher eat with such scum?" Would anyone complain about the people you're sitting with?

— DC

REACHING THE POOR AND THE OPPRESSED WITHIN YOUR community with the love of Jesus will quite often mean stepping out of your comfort zone and loving people who don't usually move within your natural social circles. Depending on where and how you grew up, you may find this challenging. You don't need to travel overseas to experience cross-cultural ministry. It can be right here in your own backyard.

The bridge that helps us cross the social disconnect we feel when reaching out of our comfort zone is our personal capacity to love those who are different to us, underpinned by our understanding of God's love for the world.

I'm not sure we fully appreciate the fullness of Jesus' mission to the entire world, even though it's stated so clearly in the most memorised scripture in the whole of the New Testament, John 3:16.

The fact Jesus didn't say, *"For God so loved the Jews…"* is startling when we consider the historical context of his statement. At a time when the Jewish people were under the rule of an occupying military empire, to declare the Father loved the *"world"* would have been at odds with the prevailing national sentiment.

> *Hey Jesus, don't you think you're being a little bit woke here? Why would you say the Father loves everyone? Surely there are those He doesn't. Heard of the Romans by any chance?*

But when did Jesus ever allow nationalistic opinion or religious bias to dictate the truth he came to teach his fellow Israelites and all future generations thereafter?

> *Later, Matthew invited Jesus and his disciples to his home as dinner guests, along with many tax collectors and other disreputable sinners. But when the Pharisees saw this, they asked his disciples, 'Why does your teacher eat with such scum?'*
>
> *When Jesus heard this, he said, 'Healthy people*

don't need a doctor—sick people do.' (Matthew 9:10-13)

Most of us find ourselves cheering Jesus on when we read this story in Matthew's gospel. We think it's a badge of honour to be known as a friend of sinners. Why? Because, as Jesus rightly pointed out, it was those who weren't well who needed a doctor. We find it difficult to understand how the Pharisees could have been so blind to their prejudice against bar owners and tax collectors, and yet we all run the risk of being just as hypocritical as the Pharisees were.

Times have changed, and to understand why the Pharisees were so upset, and why the actions of Jesus were so radical, we have to contextualise it—we have to bring it forward into our current cultural and religious settings and find something that will illicit the same response from modern-day Pharisees that Jesus faced back in his day.

That isn't an easy task, but I wholeheartedly believe it's something we *MUST* do if we're to truly understand Jesus' heart for all of humanity and not miss the lessons he has for us when blinded by our own prejudices.

If we were to read this passage in Matthew and change tax collectors and sinners to gay and transgender people, I wonder how many Christians would find themselves sitting with the Pharisees rather than the people Jesus came to reach?

I wonder how many people would push back, say it's different, then try to justify their stance with Scripture? Because don't think for a moment the Pharisees weren't justifying their aversion to the people Jesus was sitting with, in the most rigorous manner possible, internally and in conversation with each other.

What did Jesus say when he noticed the Pharisees getting upset?

> *Now go and learn the meaning of this Scripture:*
> *'I want you to show love, not offer sacrifices.'*
> (Matthew 9:13)

He took that straight from the writings of Hosea, a prophet from their history, whom the Pharisees revered.

> *I want you to show love, not offer sacrifices. I*
> *want you to know me more than I want burnt*
> *offerings.* (Hosea 6:6)

So let me ask you a confronting question. Would

anyone complain about the people you're sitting with?

If we're to reach the people Jesus sat with, we need to view them as Jesus did, not through a religious or cultural lens. If we do that, we'll find ourselves at times sitting with people who would never darken the doorway of our church.... at this point in time.

Now wouldn't that make Jesus smile?

Pastors, *one last point—it was Matthew who told this story, not Jesus...*

CHAPTER 11

WHAT'S THE OFFSHOOT OF DOING GOOD WORKS IN YOUR COMMUNITY?

When the church is known for its good works in the community, the gospel flourishes. When it's known for anything else, it struggles.

— DC

For even the Son of Man did not come to be served, but to serve, and to give his life as a ransom for many. (Mark 10:45)

AS I'VE PREVIOUSLY MENTIONED, WHEN WE FIRST arrived in Rokeby, we decided not to start any programs but instead to find out what our community was already doing and offer to help. We took Jesus' words in Mark 10 to heart and decided, rather than promoting our church throughout our community, we'd roll up our sleeves and offer to serve the various groups already doing great things in Clarence Plains.

That initially involved me, as the senior pastor, attending lots of community-led meetings because I was the one who had the time available during the week to show up. But it was here that I noticed something special happening—when the senior pastor of the local church attends community meetings, it's as if the entire church is there. The community felt that *ALL* of our church was behind them because I showed up.

Over time, we became increasingly embedded in our community, and whenever there were community-planned events, we were there, serving on committees and volunteering in practical ways. We're now known throughout Clarence Plains as a church that cares, and we've had doors open to us with people of influence simply because we did what Jesus has called us to do—help those who are in need.

> *An unexpected bonus of taking this approach was that the burden of running programs in our community wasn't carried by us. When you have limited people resource, that can be incredibly draining on a church. We were able to help lots of people outside the church without having to run events to reach them, and because we were there to help, it made connecting so much easier.*

Program burnout is a real thing in many of our churches, but it's not the program itself that burns out; it's the people running them who hit a wall and can't continue. The beauty of adopting a service-based strategy is that it's not dependent on numbers. Just one person from your church joining in to help a local group can be hugely impactful. And the weight of running the program is carried by someone else, you're just there to help.

An important consideration in making this approach work for us has been to set aside the idea that we were doing this to grow our church, and instead approach our service as our way of doing good deeds in obedience to Jesus' commands in Matthew 5 and 25.

One of the issues we were trying to address by taking this approach was that, too often, the good we do in our community is motivated by a desire for something in return—their souls. By doing that, we make our love transactional, effectively negating our loving service and turning it into a marketing strategy to grow our consumer base—where we do acts of service as a means to an end, rather than as an end in itself. I'm being really blunt here to make a point; hang in there.

I get it, it's never that clear-cut because we're all a grab bag of different motives. But we need to be aware of the *underlying* motivation behind our service if we're to avoid being seen by our community as inauthentic or opportunistic.

When you choose to do good in your local community, Jesus' love will be evident in your actions. When you love your community with no strings attached, with their best interests at heart, they'll start to see what God's love for them is really like. For that to happen, we need to go sit with them, hear their needs, and partner with them to see those needs met. When we do that, we're working for their benefit, not our own. Loving others is evidence of true discipleship.

Just in case you missed it...

In my experience, most pastors struggle with how to reach their local community. The common thought is that they have to run events to invite community members to, or run programs with a hook to get people through the door. That can be overwhelming for a young pastor who isn't a natural event planner. And the truth is, most aren't.

It also puts pressure on church members to participate and can create unhealthy expectations, leaving people feeling guilty for not contributing at the level they believe leadership expects.

Looking for ways to serve instead of starting up programs

The beauty of taking a service approach is that you're not starting up programs or running events yourself to get people to come to you. You're going out to your community and helping them with the events and programs they're already running.

> *When you offer to serve at events or in programs that your community is already invested in, they're always happy to have you there, and it's so much easier to build healthy relationships with others when you're volunteering together.*

You can take this approach as a new church plant with only a few people, or as an established church with lots of members. Size doesn't matter. Taking a service approach will help to reinforce the message to your church that all people are valuable to God and that loving them through good deeds is what Jesus is looking for from his followers.

It starts with the Pastor and leaders

> *Then Jesus said to the crowds and to his disciples, 'The teachers of religious law and the Pharisees are the official interpreters of the law of Moses. So practice and obey whatever they tell you, but don't follow their example. For they don't practice what they teach. They crush people with unbearable religious demands and never lift a finger to ease the burden.' (Matthew 23:1-4)*

Pastors, *if your people were to follow your day-to-day example, would your community be reached over the next 10 years? I'm not saying saved, but reached. If not, why not?*

 IF JESUS BUILT THE CHURCH

CHAPTER 12

SUNDAY SERVICES —THEY'RE THE CHANGE SHEDS, NOT THE MAIN GAME

"Welcome to the change sheds. What you see around you isn't what church is all about."

— DC

THIS IS HOW I STARTED A MESSAGE TO OUR CHURCH A while back....

Welcome to the change sheds. What you see around you isn't what church is all about. Where you've come from and where you're going after you leave this place today is what the church is all about. What we do on Sundays isn't the church's mission. What you do during your week is.

This is just a moment in time where you come in off the field and get to have a breather before going back out to play. Your mission is out there; it's not in here.

As the senior pastor, I'm just part of the support team

who are working hard to see you fixed up and ready to go again.

You are the church; what you see around you isn't. It's just a break in play. The game isn't played in the change sheds; it's played out on the field.

Denying self, taking up your cross daily and following Jesus (the hallmark of true discipleship), is all about what happens out there, not in here. And if you don't understand how important your day-to-day life is, in comparison to what happens here each Sunday, you'll hamstring your effectiveness for Jesus and won't make the necessary changes out there that you need to be making. You'll think that everything hinges on how well you perform when we gather together for our meetings or when you're doing other things that are considered "spiritual."

It is far more important to the kingdom of God and your relationship with Jesus that you turn up for your family, to your work, to your school, each Monday ready to lay your life down for the people in your world than whether the song leader hit the right notes or the preacher threw in a Greek word or two in his sermon on the weekend.

Now obviously, for the coach and the coaching team, what happens in the sheds and team meetings is important, but for everyone out there watching us, it's what happens on the field that's critical. Jesus isn't particularly worried about what's happening in the shed as long as his team is playing well on the field because the game isn't won in the shed, it's won on the field. And if things are going well on the field during the week, then things are more likely to be going well in the shed when we get there on Sunday.

What happens in the shed isn't seen, but what happens on the field is.

You are far more important than I am in carrying out Jesus's mission here in Hobart. I'm just a supporting character; you're the main event. I'm part of the coaching staff; you're a player on the field. And before you say Jesus is the main character (I get it), you need to realise that he's chosen to reach the world with his love, through you.

CHAPTER 13

LOOKING AT OUR BUILDINGS DIFFERENTLY

If we spend the majority of our treasure on ourselves,
what good have we achieved?

— DC

As far back as I can remember, in Bible college, we were taught that owning your own church building was a strategic Kingdom investment. We were told that owning land was like driving a stake into the ground for the Kingdom of God and carried great spiritual weight in claiming ground from the kingdom of darkness.

But is any of this really true, and if there's truth contained in those thoughts, should they be the priority of our treasure?

There's no doubt having a church building in a town is a tangible representation of religion, but does it really do all that we've been led to believe, or is it a distraction from the main game?

There could be an argument for older-style cathedrals being a showcase for the magnificence of God, but how does it stack up against the humble carpenter from Nazareth who claimed no home of his own?

Nowadays, many of us can't use the cathedral argument, as most of our churches look more like modern-day convention centres than temples to God.

"But it's not a temple", you'd say. *"We're the temple of God"*, and you'd be right. But you then have to ask yourself this question:

> *If buildings aren't needed by God to extend his kingdom across the earth because it's his followers who do that, why do we devote so much time, treasure and talent to them?*

For most churches, property management is our biggest expense, aside from salaries. The question, then, is:

"Who is our property for?"

The problem with church buildings is the message they send to our community every day of the week. They tell our community we value ourselves more than we value them. A little harsh? Possibly, but it's good to think about it from their perspective.

If it's only the things we give away during our lives that we take with us into eternity, why do we tie up so much of our treasure in buildings for ourselves when those buildings could be so much more?

What if we were to make our buildings our gift to our local community, not just our Sunday home?

In November 2015, our church bought an old, run-down pub in Rokeby. We decided right from the start that we wouldn't hold services at the pub, but would instead develop it into a meeting hub for our local community and offer it to them for their benefit. We coined the phrase "The Grace Centre – Our gift to our community," to keep our vision front and centre. We took our treasure, and we spent it on our community. Today, we're known as a church that cares for its community. Why? Because our community has seen what we've spent our treasure on, and they've come to that conclusion. What do you think that tells them about the One we serve and His heart toward them?

What has happened at the Grace Centre has been extraordinary, but this chapter isn't about our story. This chapter is to challenge you to rethink your thoughts about your church building.

If people in your community were to look at what you've spent your treasure on, what would they say is the focus of your church?

If you have a building, then there's Exhibit A for everyone to see. Why not change the focus of your building from being your home to being your gift to your community? It would make all the difference to them.

CHAPTER 14

WHERE TO FROM HERE?

Your church is already reaching its community because your people live there.

— DC

I TITLED THE LAST CHAPTER OF THIS BOOK "WHERE TO from here?" but it's a bit of a misnomer, because I'm probably leaving you with more questions than answers.

The truth is, for you to get the most out of this book and see it change you and your church, you need to sit with the things that have stirred you and challenged your practice, and allow the Holy Spirit to bring clarity and direction for you personally.

I want you to picture this book as a great big sign with these words written on it,

"These are some of the things you need to seriously consider as you follow Jesus and lead others along the narrow path that leads to life."

What you discover on that path will become your story and, God willing, part of the unfolding story of His worldwide Church.

This next point will go a long way to alleviating the burden that far too many pastors carry.

Your church is *already* reaching its community.

How do I know that? Because your people live in a community every day of their week. It probably won't be the community your church building is situated in, because nowadays people often drive to church and could be living a long way away in a totally different suburb. But they're already present in *their* community throughout the week.

The first priority for your church members should always be the community they naturally find themselves in from Monday to Sunday. Your responsibility is to equip them to love the people in their community better—whether that's their extended family, their workplace, school, or local neighbourhood.

So, take a deep breath and relax, you're already engaged and involved in reaching the lost.

Secondly, realise that anything you do as a church to reach the community your Sunday meeting is located in, is a bonus. It should never take the place of each believer's personal responsibility towards the people in *their* world.

In our church, I always tell our members that their first and most important responsibility as believers is the community they naturally find themselves in during the week, and then, if they have any margin left over, they can assist us with what we're doing at the Grace Centre. Most of our church isn't involved in a hands-on way, and that's totally fine, because the Grace Centre isn't the mission of our church. Making disciples who obey the commands of Jesus in their day-to-day lives is.

So, if our church members are growing in their obedience to love others in the same way that Jesus loves them, then I'm completely satisfied because I know they'll hear Jesus say, *"Well done, good and faithful servant"*, when they stand before him.

The Grace Centre isn't our church's priority; it's mine because that's where I work during the week. I've never asked our church to do something that I'm not willing to do myself. I consider what's happened at the Grace Centre over the past 10 years an object lesson in what can happen when any of God's people seek to serve the community they find them-selves in, in their day-to-day lives.

If you make the church's corporate activity their first priority, you take them down a path that can lead to burnout and disappointment. That doesn't mean that your people can't come together to do something that they can't do on their own. But it should flow from a meeting of hearts and intent, rather than a top-down directive driven by leadership who have a bunch of KPIs, vaguely disguised as vision, that they want to tick off.

Okay, moving right along…

I was with a group of Christian leaders, and we were discussing some of the ideas that are in this book. Near the end of our time together, one of the pastors asked a question that stumped me at first. They said, *"Well, how are we supposed to love others? You've convinced us that love is key, but how do we do it?"*

To be honest, the reason the question surprised me at the time was the fact that it was asked in the first place. If this is all that Jesus has commanded us to do—love others as he has loved us, which then proves our love for him—surely those who have the sacred responsibility of leading the church should have it figured out already. I mean, we're only talking about the red words of Jesus here, not the entire Bible.

But it got me thinking. I decided to take another look at what Jesus said about loving others, and I came across something interesting. Jesus didn't give prescriptive instructions.

There were two things that he said that stood out to me.

They were, *"Do to others as you would have them do to you"* (Luke 6:31, Matthew 7:12) and *"Love your neighbour as yourself."* (Matthew 22:39, Mark 12:31).

Interestingly, Jesus added the same observation to each of these statements—*when we put them into practice, we fulfil all of the law and the prophets.*

They both require us to think about our response from a personal perspective and then act accordingly. We're required to place ourselves in the shoes of others and then ask, *"What would I like them to do for me if I were in their situation?"* And then we do it.

Why would Jesus take that approach? After all, he could have been very explicit and explained it step by step, but he didn't. In fact, you won't find a playbook anywhere in the New Testament that gives you step-by-step instructions on how to walk love out.

> *There is something about identifying with those who need our care that is good for them and good for us.*

A great question I've taught our church to ask themselves in any situation where they don't know what to do, is:

"What would love do?"

Sometimes love says *"yes"* and sometimes love says *"no."*

Now, just for a moment, I want you to imagine something with me. What if the church today wasn't known by any of our negative history—our institutionalised church structures that reward performance before heart, our vast property holdings that seem to fly in the face of Jesus' teaching about earthly treasure, our strange and/or archaic meetings, our sordid sexual past, our collusion with political power and our judgement of others—but rather by our acts of kindness specifically to the poor and the oppressed. What if our entire reputation in the eyes of the world was built around our loving service to those that the rest of society shuns, and the use of our treasure to meet the needs of the hungry and the homeless?

> *Imagine what it would be like if this was the way the entire body of Christ functioned; if Matthew 25 was the goal that every believer aspired to. How do you think the world would view us? How do you think the world would view the One we follow?*

Would our world be different today if it had experienced 2000 years of that type of church?

Our world *is* different today, but only because there have always been believers within the church who, since Pentecost, have given their lives to following Jesus' commands. But it could have been so much more if we hadn't been sidetracked with being the head and not the tail, chasing after the powerful rather than serving the *"least of these"*.

> *If you listen to these commands of the Lord your God that I am giving you today, and if you carefully obey them, the Lord will make you the head and not the tail, and you will always be on top and never at the bottom.* (Deuteronomy 28:13)

Whilst God did give a promise to the Israelites on the way to the promised land, there was a condition attached. They had to obey all that he had commanded them. And then HE would promote them. They were never told to seek promotion themselves.

When we make being the *head and not the tail* the goal, and being *on top and never at the bottom* our expected ministry outcome when serving Jesus, is it any wonder we miss the clear instructions that Jesus gave to deny ourselves and prioritise the hungry, the thirsty, the naked, the homeless, the sick and those in prison?

Imagine if we could forget about ourselves and live our lives in service to the poor and the oppressed—the whole world would sit up and take notice, and God would be seen throughout the entire earth, just as Jesus said would happen in Matthew 5:16. That's my dream, and I believe it's the dream of the Holy Spirit as well.

Well, all good things must come to an end, but I'm not going to drop you like a hot potato now that I've finished writing. I've added a bonus section of questions for each chapter to help you process what you've just read. You can go through them individually or collectively as a team, and they'll help you with your thinking around some of the challenging issues we've tackled in the book.

Finally, let me close with something I said right at the start.

> *It's totally okay if you disagree with some of what's been written in this book, but if it helps you think more clearly about your practice, then my goal will have been achieved. We're all pilgrims on a journey, and what one sees, another may not. Don't be afraid to ask questions, even if you feel you're disrespecting a sacred cow. We all see dimly as through a dark glass, but we have this confidence that the Holy Spirit will lead us into all truth. So, let's not stumble over the stones*

in the road but instead press on to take hold of all that Jesus has for us.

"You can tell whether a man is clever by his answers. You can tell whether a man is wise by his questions." Mahfouz Naguib

"All changes, even the most longed for, have their melancholy; for what we leave behind us is a part of ourselves; we must die to one life before we can enter another." Anatole France

DISCUSSION QUESTIONS FOR INDIVIDUAL OR GROUP REFLECTION

This could very well be the most valuable section of my entire book. Whilst reading the book is good, most of what you read will be forgotten shortly after. It's only the things that you grapple with and think through for yourself that have any chance of changing your perspective and consequently your practice of ministry and life.

As you may have noticed, I love questions. Asking the right questions has been invaluable in my personal walk with Jesus and addressing my own blind spots in my practice.

Here are a few that could be useful in helping you and your team gain even more value from my writing.

These questions are designed for personal reflection, small group discussion, or leadership team conversations. Don't rush through them. Sit with the uncomfortable ones. Let the Holy Spirit do His work.

Remember, none of us sees everything perfectly. We all have our blind spots. Let's commit to authenticity and humility in our practice. I know that if we do, God's truth will become increasingly clear for all of us.

QUESTIONS: WAITING ON GOD—IT WILL CHANGE YOUR LIFE!

1. The author spent 6 years going to the botanical gardens every Monday to wait on God in silence. What would it take for you to commit to something similar?

2. *"Rather than telling God what I thought He should do, I found it far wiser to simply hold that person or situation before Him."* How is that different from how you normally pray?

3. What *"residue of sin, pain, disappointment and weariness"* has built up in your life from ministry or just from life? What would it mean to you if waiting on God was able to clean it out?

4. *"He's waiting to be wanted."* When was the last time you simply wanted to be with God, not because you needed something, but just to be with Him?

5. How might waiting on God in silence
   change the way you approach ministry,
   relationships, and the challenges you face?

QUESTIONS: THE EMPEROR HAS NO CLOTHES

1. When was the last time you actually spent time with someone who was poor or disadvantaged? If you can't remember, what does that tell you about your proximity to the people Jesus prioritised?

2. *"We speak a big game, but the substance is too often lacking."* That's a tough statement. Where do you see the gap between what we say we believe and what we actually do and experience?

3. Have you been praying for revival? What exactly are you expecting to happen? How will you know if God answers that prayer?

4. *"I'm not waiting for a move of God; I am a move of God."* Does that statement by William Booth excite you or make you uncomfortable? Why?

5. Peter remembered that Jesus went around *"doing good"* before he mentioned the miracles. Why do you think that was Peter's first memory? What does your church or your life lead with?

6. If the Holy Spirit's anointing is primarily for reaching the poor and oppressed, what does that mean for how we should be using our spiritual gifts?

QUESTIONS: ANOINTED TO TAKE GOOD NEWS TO THE POOR

1. Jesus linked his anointing by the Holy Spirit directly to his mission to the poor. How does that challenge the way you've thought about the Holy Spirit's work in your life?

2. Why don't the poor receive *"top billing"* when pastors gather to discuss ministry? Why haven't you attended a conference or training where the poor were the priority?

3. The author suggests that maybe our lack of miracles isn't because of a lack of passion for the gifts, but a lack of obedience to reach the poor. Does that thought make you defensive or does it ring true?

4. Read Matthew 25:31-46 again slowly. Now sit with it. Don't rush past it. What does this passage actually say you'll be judged on? How does that make you feel?

5. Isaiah 58 is brutal in its honesty about religious activity that doesn't lead to helping the poor. Can you identify any religious activities in your own life or church that might fall into this category?

6. *"If the alleviation of poverty and injustice doesn't feature prominently in your teaching and practice in your local church, you're in danger of becoming a Pharisee."* That's confronting. How prominently does it feature in your church? In your personal life?

QUESTIONS: WHY SHOULD THE CHURCH FOCUS ON THE POOR?

1. The author talks about cultural blind spots —individualism and materialism. Can you identify these values operating in your own life? How do they conflict with Jesus' teaching?

2. When Jesus says, *"sell your possessions and give to the poor,"* what's your first internal response? Be honest about the fear or resistance you feel.

3. Can you name someone you know personally who would fit the statistics about poverty in Australia (3.3 million people living in poverty, 1 in 6 children)? If not, how can you reach people you don't even know exist?

4. *"Poverty that results from injustice and exploitation is the most visible and striking sign of the sin of the world."* Do you agree? Does

seeing poverty this way change how you think about addressing it?

5. The author lists numerous Old Testament passages about God's heart for the poor. Why do you think we skip over these so easily in our teaching and preaching?

6. *"Whoever is kind to the poor lends to the LORD, and he will reward them for what they have done." The poor can't reward you, but He will.* How does that shift your motivation for serving?

QUESTIONS:
THE PASTOR'S
RESPONSIBILITY
TOWARD THEIR FLOCK

1. What do you want to hear Jesus say when you stand before him? Now, based on Matthew 25, what will you actually hear?

2. *"It's easy, we need to teach our people that our salvation is dependent on both faith and good works."* Does that statement make you nervous? Why does the church shy away from talking about works?

3. Read Romans 2:5-8, Matthew 25:46, and James 2:14-24. How do these passages challenge a "faith alone" understanding of salvation?

4. *"Your good deeds cannot open the door of salvation; only Jesus can. But once it's open, it's your good deeds that will keep it from closing."* Does this balance make sense to you?

5. Hebrews 10:24 says to *"think of ways to motivate one another to acts of love and good works."* How much time in your church services is devoted to this versus other priorities?

6. *"Pastor, don't skip over verse 24 and go straight to verse 25."* Why do we focus so much on *"not neglecting to meet together"* (v25) but ignore motivating people to good works (v24)?

QUESTIONS: WHAT WE MEASURE, WE START TO VALUE

1. Make a list of what your church actually measures (attendance, giving, volunteers, small groups, etc.). Now make a list of what Jesus said he'd measure us by (feeding the hungry, clothing the naked, visiting prisoners, etc.). How do those lists compare?

2. Have you ever felt like a *"failure"* as a Christian because you weren't bringing people to church? Where did that pressure come from?

3. *"When we stand in front of Jesus, he won't be asking us for our tithe or our attendance records."* How does that statement make you feel—relieved? Confronted? Sceptical?

4. What's the difference between measuring church success and measuring faithfulness to Jesus' commands? Which is easier? Which matters more?

5. If you stopped measuring bums on seats
   and started measuring the good works your
   congregation was doing for the poor, how
   would your church have to change?

QUESTIONS: IS IT BETTER TO REACH BEFORE YOU PREACH?

1. *"How do you go into all the world? You don't do it by praying, and you don't do it by preaching. They're the bookends to the "go" part. You do it by reaching the community you've been planted in and letting them experience something that they've never experienced before—the love of God as expressed through our good works"* Does that statement bother you? Why or why not?

2. The author's church decided to find out what the community was already doing and offer to help rather than starting their own programs. What would that look like in your context? What makes that approach exciting?

3. *"When you truly try to serve your community with no strings attached, doors will open for you without you having to knock."* Have you

experienced this? If so, why do you think that was the case?

4. Be honest—do you serve with *"no strings attached"* or are you hoping for conversions? What's the difference between those two motivations?

5. How would your church have to change if you hired a school hall for Sunday services and gave your building away as a gift to your community? What does your reaction to that idea tell you?

6. *"The world isn't looking for a successful, powerful, all-conquering church. The world is looking for a church that looks like Jesus, our servant King."* Do you agree? What does a church that looks like Jesus actually look like in practice?

QUESTIONS: MY DILEMMA WITH DISCIPLESHIP

1. Have you been taught that every Christian's responsibility is to *"make disciples"*? How has that teaching affected your sense of success or failure as a believer?

2. The author argues that making disciples may be a calling for some, but not for all. Does that idea feel like relief or like he's lowering the bar?

3. *"Not many of you should become teachers"* (James 3:1). If teaching is essential to making disciples, how does James's warning fit with the idea that everyone should be making disciples?

4. Read Matthew 25:31-46 one more time. What will Jesus actually judge your life on? How does that compare to what you thought being a "good Christian" required?

5. If the primary responsibility of every
   believer is to love those who can't repay
   them (the poor, sick, imprisoned), how
   would your daily life need to change?

6. *"Pastors, don't fall into the trap of preaching
   your job description to your congregation."*
   Have you experienced this? How does it
   create unnecessary guilt and burnout?

QUESTIONS: IT'S FAR SIMPLER THAN YOU THINK

1. Jesus summed up discipleship as loving God and loving others. Why do we make it so much more complicated than that?

2. *"A disciple is someone who obeys the commands of Christ."* What are the actual commands of Christ (not the bylaws of your church)? List them.

3. The author says typical discipleship programs focus on reading the Bible, praying daily, attending church, tithing, and volunteering—but Jesus won't judge any of those things. How does that challenge your current approach to discipleship?

4. *"Any Christian I've ever known who has actively placed loving others as their primary goal in life does all of the rest anyway."* Have you found this to be true? Why or why not?

5. When church leadership focuses on Sunday services instead of helping people love better, what happens to the mission of the church?

6. *"Service is simply love in action."* Where in your life are you actively stepping down to serve others with Jesus' love, the way he stepped down from heaven to serve you?

QUESTIONS: WHO WOULD JESUS SIT WITH?

1. Matthew was a tax collector, and Jesus ate with "disreputable sinners." Who are the equivalent people in our culture today that would make religious people uncomfortable?

2. The author updates the Matthew 9 passage to include gay and transgender people. What was your gut reaction to reading that? Be honest about it.

3. *"I want you to show love, not offer sacrifices."* How do we sometimes hide behind religious activity instead of actually loving people who make us uncomfortable?

4. How do we balance truth and love when it comes to people whose lifestyles we believe are sinful? What did Jesus model for us?

5. Would anyone complain about the people

you're sitting with? If not, are you sitting
where Jesus would sit?

Questions: Who would Jesus sit with?

QUESTIONS: WHAT'S THE OFFSHOOT OF DOING GOOD WORKS IN YOUR COMMUNITY?

1. *"When you actively serve your community through your good works, your community will open its heart to you."* Have you experienced this? Or have you only tried to get the community to come to you?

2. Grace Church served on committees and volunteered at community events without running their own programs. What fears would you have about taking that approach? (Be honest—fear of irrelevance? Fear of losing control? Fear of not getting credit?)

3. *"Where we did acts of service as a means to an end rather than an end in itself."* Can you identify times when your service has been transactional—expecting souls in exchange for your help?

4. What would *"loving with no strings attached"* actually look like in your community? How is that different from what you're currently doing?

5. *"Pastor, if your people were to follow your day-to-day example, would your community be reached (not saved but reached) over the next 10 years?"* Pastors, answer honestly. Everyone else, to what extent would your community be reached if people followed your example?

QUESTIONS: SUNDAY SERVICES—THEY'RE THE CHANGE SHEDS, NOT THE MAIN GAME

1. *"Welcome to the change sheds. What you see around you isn't what church is all about."* How does thinking about Sunday services this way change your perspective on their importance?

2. If Sunday is just the halftime break and the real game is played Monday through Saturday, how does that shift your priorities for the week?

3. *"You are far more important than I am when it comes to seeing the mission of Jesus being carried out."* Do you believe that? Or do you think the pastor/leaders are the "real" ministers?

4. What would change in your church if everyone understood that their Monday

through Saturday life was more important
than their Sunday morning performance?

5. How much of your spiritual energy goes
    into what happens in the "shed" versus what
    happens on the "field"? What does that ratio
    tell you?

QUESTIONS: LOOKING AT OUR BUILDINGS DIFFERENTLY

1. *"If we spend the majority of our treasure on ourselves, what good have we achieved?"* Look at your church budget. What percentage goes to buildings/property versus directly to serving the poor?

2. "Church buildings tell our community that we value ourselves more than we value them." Is that a fair statement? Why or why not?

3. What if you made your church building your gift to your community instead of your Sunday home? What would that require? What would you lose? What might you gain?

4. *"You don't tell people how to use the gift you've given them."* How hard would it be to truly give your building away to the community with no strings attached?

5. If people in your community looked at what you've spent your treasure on, what would they say is the focus of your church?

   Questions: Looking at our buildings differently

FINAL REFLECTION QUESTIONS

1. How did you feel when the author said your church was already active in community engagement? Did it take a burden off your shoulders? How does it change the way you think about mission when you realise your people are already involved?

2. Of all the chapters, which one made you most uncomfortable? Why? What is that discomfort trying to tell you?

3. What's one concrete thing you could do this week to move toward the poor, the marginalised, or the forgotten in your community?

4. If you were to measure your faithfulness by Jesus' standards (Matthew 25) instead of typical church standards, how would you be doing?

5. What would need to change in your church
    for it to become so integral to your
    community that if you closed your doors,
    your community would suffer?

6. *"It's totally okay if you disagree with some of
    what's been written in this book, but if it helps
    you think more clearly about your practice,
    then that's a good thing."* What parts did you
    disagree with? What parts are you still
    wrestling with? What's one thing you know
    you need to change?

            Final reflection questions

RESOURCES

Allen, K. A. (2019). Making sense of belonging. *InPsych, 41* (3). Accessed from: https://www.psychol ogy.org.au/for-members/publications/inpsych/2019/ june/Making-sense-of-belonging

Christian Jayakumar (2014) God of the Empty-Handed: Poverty, Power and the Kingdom of God. Acorn Press

Hwa Yung. (2021) Leadership or Servanthood? Walking in the Steps of Jesus Langham Global Library

Kreider, Alan (2016) The Patient Ferment of the Early Church: The Improbable Rise of Christianity in the Roman Empire. Publisher: Baker Academic

Kroger, J. (2017). Identity development in adolescence and adulthood. *Oxford Research Encyclopaedia of Psychology.* from

https://oxfordre.com/psychology/view/10.1093/acre fore/9780190236557.001.0001/acrefore-9780190236557-e-54.

Myers, Bryant (2011). Walking with the Poor: Principles and Practices of Transformational Development ORBIS Publisher

New International Version (NIV): Zondervan. (2011). *The Holy Bible: New International Version.* Zondervan.

New Living Translation (NLT): Tyndale House Publishers. (2015). *The Holy Bible: New Living Translation.* Tyndale House Publishers.

Portal, Pete. (2023) *How to Be (Un)Successful.* Publisher: Form.

Wright, Christopher (2020) Shaping a Missional Hermeneutic – The Mission of God

Wu, Siu Fung (2009) Good News to the Poor – Another Way to Love: Christian Social Reform and Global Poverty

ABOUT THE AUTHOR

Dermot Cottuli

Dermot is a seasoned pastor and church leader with over 37 years of experience in Christian ministry, including youth ministry and senior pastoral roles from North Queensland to Tasmania.

He currently serves as the Senior Pastor of Grace Church Clarence Plains, where he and his wife, Debra, have led their local faith community for more than two decades.

Passionate about seeing the church deeply embedded in its community, Dermot champions a model of ministry that prioritises service over programs, believing the love of Jesus is best expressed through authentic, grassroots engagement rather than traditional church metrics.

His writing and teaching explore innovative approaches to church practice, leadership, community engagement, and discipleship, challenging conventional assumptions and inviting others to think more deeply about the church's role in society.

Through his teaching and writing, Dermot challenges traditional assumptions about church success and leadership, encouraging believers to measure faithfulness by impact rather than size. *"If your church disappeared tomorrow,"* he asks, *"would your community even notice?"*

This question has shaped much of his pastoral vision and continues to guide his work. Dermot and Debra live in Tasmania and have four adult children and a cat.

https://ifjesusbuiltthechurch.com/